RAISING TROUBLED KIDS
Help for Parents of Children
with Mental Illness or Emotional Disorders

Margaret Puckette

TO MY LOVELY DAUGHTERS

TABLE OF CONTENTS

ALL ILLUSTRATIONS BY THE AUTHOR.

ACKNOWLEDGMENTS

A book like this is never written alone. It depends on dozens of families and children to tell their difficult stories; it depends on the author's supportive family and friends; and it depends on the advice and counsel of mental health professionals who work with children. First and foremost, I must thank my father, Bud Schauerte, who supported me emotionally during my many hard parenting years, and then encouraged me to write a book about the experience so that others could benefit. Furthermore, he persisted with gentle reminders for at least *a decade* before I finally sat down and got started!

I send copious thanks to my editor, Susan Spitzer, for her professionalism and careful review of the text. Thanks also go to my readers, Dr. Elizabeth Hamilton and Lisa Heigh, for their general comments on the book's clarity and focus. Important input came from the psychiatrists and therapeutic staff at Trillium Family Services in Portland, OR, which validated the treatment approaches used in this book, and gave me the professionals' perspective on how families can best work with providers.

All anecdotes are from actual experiences as shared by parents, siblings, grandparents, foster parents, and by troubled children themselves—real people who lived through, and survived, the challenges of mental disorders. *Thank you.* I hope your stories will have a ripple effect that will spread far and wide to help many others like you.

The family stories were collected over a decade by visitors to my family support group. For many, family support groups are a lifesaver, and the affirmation and advice people receive from other families helps them turn their lives around. My group was provided free to the general public thanks to the group's sponsors: first, the Accountable Behavioral Health Alliance in Corvallis, Oregon, from 1999 to 2004, and then, the Jean Baton Swindells Center for Children and Families at Providence Hospital in Portland, Oregon from 2005 to present. I also thank the families I worked with as a family partner for Trillium Family Services, then for Wraparound Oregon of Multnomah County.

INTRODUCTION

My story

When one of my children was fifteen, I found out that she had been having hallucinations for at least two years, but was able to hide the fact from everyone until the visions and voices became so overpowering that she could no longer concentrate or pay attention in her classes. This was the beginning of the most difficult years of life for her as for all of the family members. As the condition became progressively worse and dangerous, we together endured a period of overwhelming stress, confusion, and loss, and all I could do was watch helplessly as everything important to me fell apart—friendships and relationships, work, finances, my health, and the well being of my children.

What was worse was being a single parent and finding little or no help. I expected understanding, but like so many other families: I was blamed instead of supported, my child was falsely accused of drug use, I was accused of being a weak parent, and I endured lots of unwanted and inappropriate advice. These messages came from close friends, family members, clergy, doctors, teachers, even mental health professionals! The blame and judgment came from so many directions that it was hard to believe they weren't true. On top of this, I felt guilty that I somehow caused my child's condition and I searched for explanations: did I do something when I was pregnant? Was their a virus or germ? Did I discipline too hard? Were family genetics involved? Had there been abuse by someone and I didn't know about it or stop it?

Like other families, I felt a deep profound grief and sense of loss. It seemed like my wonderful child had 'died', and that she would never be the same and her future would be bleak. It probably feels this way for families with a child with cancer or leukemia or other dangerous chronic condition—one never knows if it will get better or get worse and worry about the future is always present. It felt so alone, as if no one else was going through the same things. It was too embarrassing to ask questions, as if it would reveal to others that my family (and I) was "messed up." Or perhaps I didn't want to find out it was true.

I grieved over my own lost dreams too. It was hard enough being single, but I now had to put my life aside, give up career plans and joyful things like hobbies or travels. I had to devote every moment to trying to hold things together. I say "*trying* to hold things together" because my family seemed to fly apart at the slightest thing. I became so weakened emotionally by stress that I became very depressed and wondered if life was worth living. I distinctly remember it was a fabulous sunny spring day when that suicidal thought occurred, the colorful roses had just bloomed, yet all I could think was "who cares? There's no joy in anything anymore." It was a wake-up call. I realized that if I didn't take care of myself, how could I care for my family that I loved so much? Therapy and a period of about 8 months on an antidepressant, finally gave me the ability to take steps to effectively nurture my family and myself.

Once better and out of my own danger zone, I read everything I could about mental illness, spoke to therapists and a psychiatrist, and joined a local mental health organization. Even after this, there was no information about how I should raise my daughter or make changes in my home to improve our stressful lives. Besides not knowing what to do, the professionals couldn't tell me anything about what to expect or a diagnosis. More frustrating, they kept information about her from me, and didn't listen to my observations or take my concerns seriously.

This is the book I wish I had had, written to help you learn what worked for me and what's worked for numerous other families with troubled children of all ages. Your family *can* manage when every day is full of stress and exhaustion. Things *will* get better. I have facilitated support groups for parents with seriously troubled children and teens for many years and there is a lot of wisdom out there, which was put in here. This book is about you, and how you can recover a stable life at home and keep it as normal as possible.

Professional care from doctors, therapists, counselors or other treatment providers is largely child-focused, not family-focused. People in the system forget that you are the ultimate "care provider" and ultimately responsible for your child's well being into their adulthood. But things are beginning to change. The good news is that research shows that competent family care has the best outcome for people with disorders in the long term.

When I first established a support group for parents in my community, the same experiences came up regardless of the family situation, the child, or the child's specific problem. It didn't matter whether the parents were together and financially able to pay for treatment, or whether the family was a single parent or relative with financial difficulties. It didn't even matter whether the child had severe symptoms or was just stable enough to attend school. The family stresses exacted a big price on many: loss of a relationship including the relationships with other children; financial hardship; job loss; loss of social supports; loss of peace of mind (depression, anxiety), and worse, loss of hope.

You can do what I and other families did and it will work. It will be hard; I cannot claim that your challenges will be over quickly or overcome easily because brain disorders are serious and disabling. But you can do it! Treatment works. Hang in there and have hope! I found out that all families go through the same things. I found out that with brain disorders in children and teens there is no quick fix and no quick diagnosis. Don't let this frustrate you. *Diagnosis is not necessary to begin treatment and see real improvement.*

A national news story motivated me to consider this book. As a desperate attempt to get help, a family in Oregon abandoned their 11-year-old daughter at a local hospital. The parents had tried repeatedly but unsuccessfully to get treatment for her serious behavior, which was so violent that the parents locked her in her room at night so that she would not be able to attack and kill her siblings or even themselves as they slept. No one took their concerns seriously. After the abandonment and the publicity on national news, there was public outcry that the parents should face criminal charges for child abandonment. However, families across the nation began writing our newspaper and speaking out that they understood how a family could go to extremes when trying to get help for a dangerous child. The story had a good ending, these parents were not charged, and their daughter received treatment thanks to an enlightened district attorney.

Since I lived in the area and was known as a family advocate, a regional newspaper contacted me for an interview to get the perspective of another parent. The reporter said the paper had been getting calls and email from across the nation for days from these other families offering solace and support for the parents. Each wanted the reporter to let the family know they had experienced the same helplessness and stress and inability to get the help they needed. The newspaper editors were overwhelmed by the response and decided to run a series of stories about children with mental illness and the children's mental health care system. It was clear that parents throughout the country went through the same things, and needed support and affirmation, and practical advice for managing their lives and reducing their stress and desperation.

෩

Key lessons in this book:

- *All families experience the same struggles, no matter what the child's diagnosis or cause of their serious behaviors.*

- *All parents and siblings (or other caregivers) have mixed feelings of guilt, anger, frustration, pain and loss.*

- *The steps to finding peace in the home are the same for all families, and they lead to nurturing and hope for all family members and to improving the troubled child's long term outcome.*

- *You can start helping yourself and your child now. You do not yet need a diagnosis for your child to begin the right steps to effective treatment and peace of mind.*

The first chapter in this book starts with the most important person: YOU. As the one who is reading this book, you are likely the one carrying a substantial burden in your family. **The absolute first priority is for you to be together emotionally and physically.** The first chapters cover how you and your family can do this, and how to build a safe healing foundation in your home. Later chapters cover information about how to manage your child's behavior and structure your home life in a way that promotes improved behavior and "recovery" from symptoms.

Your competent parenting skills will be critical to guiding your child to a functional adulthood.

TERMINOLOGY

Children with mental or emotional disorders and their families are incredibly diverse, and the text describes situations that apply to all types of families and all types of children, regardless of family structure, the type of disorder of the child, or the severity of the behavior. A family can be any close group of people who live and share together, regardless of whether there are: one or two parents in the home, one or more children, or whether everyone is biologically related. But to keep the text simple and easy to follow, the following terms will be used throughout:

TROUBLED CHILD – The child or teen with overwhelmingly difficult behavior due to any cause or reason, regardless of age or gender. The child may have a diagnosed mental illness, may use street drugs or alcohol, or may act out with frightening, destructive, or irrational behaviors for some other reason.

TROUBLED BEHAVIOR – Anything to excess that prevents the child from managing at school, maintaining good friends, and respecting themselves or others. The behavior feels abnormal and can range from complete withdrawal from the world to aggression or violence. The child does not develop emotionally like their peers and shows few natural instincts like a desire for self-preservation. Stressful situations will aggravate the behavior and nothing seems to improve it. They seem to always need more: more help, more control, more attention, more rescues.

"NORMAL" BEHAVIOR – Commonly expected behavior or a child or young adult that develops intellectually and emotionally over time, and keeps up with the development of their peers. A normal child has friendships with other "normal" children, has natural instincts for self-preservation, moderated feelings and actions, and an ability to recover from stressful situations.

SPOUSE – This can mean any important adult in the household, a partner, stepparent, grandparent, or other co-habitant. For a single parent this might apply to others who know your family, see you regularly, and provide significant emotional support to you and any of your children.

CARE PROVIDER – A term that refers to those who are paid to help your troubled child: a school counselor, doctor, psychologist or psychiatrist, therapist, and others in the mental health and addiction treatment fields.

COMMUNITY – If it takes a village to raise a child, it takes a very special village to help the family of that child. Your community consists of the people you see or interact with regularly such as the extended family, a religious congregation, neighbors, co-workers and teachers. Among these will be several generous honest souls who volunteer to help your family in difficult times.

RECOVERY – Recovery is an interesting term. It is used to describe someone with a chronic mental or emotional disorder that functions as well or the same as everyone else. They are mentally healthy but *not cured*, per se, it means they manage and control their symptoms with therapy, coping skills, medication, and stress reduction techniques. Being "in recovery" requires a lifetime of discipline and habit. Note that the term "recovery" is also used to describe an alcoholic that stops drinking and doesn't start again. The recovering alcoholic will always have the addiction, but avoids drinking with discipline and support from others.

What does recovery look like - *A "recovered" person with a mental or emotional disorder looks and acts like everyone else. They have healthy relationships or friendships, a steady job, and they handle everyday life responsibilities such as maintaining a place to live, eating normally, keeping themselves and their clothing clean, and taking responsibility for their actions. Recovery happens when the person pays attention to themselves to notice if the symptoms are starting, and then takes action to stop the symptoms.*

CHAPTER 1
You are not alone.

There are families throughout the world that include a child that just "isn't right in the head." This child's behavior is difficult, frightening, or stressful to others, and the child can't or doesn't improve. It's common enough that everyone knows a family with a child like this. Ask around. The child's serious behaviors stand out so glaringly, that it makes the child's family stand out too. If people aren't aware that some children are born with brain problems or develop them around puberty, they may speculate what's wrong with the child. Many will try to help but don't understand, and many will attribute this child's problems to the family. It is common for families to start keeping things to themselves.

Inside your home, it feels like your world is caving in, that every day is a struggle, and that things are getting worse no matter what you do. Families like yours endure stress in many forms, and are completely drained by their efforts to live day-to-day with chaos and stress. You also feel alone and different. You don't see other families going through these same things.

The parenting problems you face are not like those of other families, but they are *normal* for families like yours: crisis after crisis, strained relationships with a spouse, friend, or another family member, exhaustion without a break, anxiety, helplessness, and sadness. And getting help may not be helpful at all, because the mental health system doesn't guide you, or health care providers and teachers don't listen to your story or trust your judgment. It's common to feel that your energy and money are being constantly drained. Everyone in your family has been sacrificing things they need or enjoy for a long time, and suffering a tremendous loss of well being.

You are not crazy.

> *"It's kind of like being in your own little war zone at home."*
> — Mother of an 8-year-old son with bipolar disorder

Stress makes you feel crazy. Because of what's been happening in your life for months or years, your stress has been building up. You've been good at holding things together but paying a price: sleepless nights, or regular illnesses, or anger.

You might be so overwhelmed by coping that you aren't noticing how this affects everyone's physical and emotional well being. Even after some people realize that stress is taking its toll, they discount its severity or feel like they can handle it. People usually try to tough things out heroically on their own, probably because they don't want to feel like a failure or think they can't handle it. But stress is likely to affect your health and thinking more than you realize. Stress affects not only you but also the rest of your family, and it especially affects your troubled child! You can reduce the stress in your life, but it's important to recognize it exists first before you can remove the stressors. Have you noticed the following signs of stress in yourself or other family members?

Signs of Stress
- Sadness and the blues that last for more than a few of weeks
- Periods of crying
- Weight loss or weight gain
- Irritability, even at small things
- Increased drinking or use of street drugs, increased "escape" activities like gambling or shopping sprees
- Sleeplessness
- Forgetfulness, losing track, feeling "spacey"
- Getting sick more often, feeling exhausted all the time
- Feeling anxious, frustrated, even when there's no specific reason

It's not your fault.

> *"People just don't understand that it's not willful, that their kid is not "choosing" to be a punk but that it's in their biology."*
> — Mother of 9-year-old with ADHD

It's common to blame yourself and feel guilty for causing your child's problems. It's also common to blame your difficult child and other family members, or to blame "the System" that's failed you and your child but it is no one's fault. Serious behavior problems happen, just like cancer and birth defects. Your child's problem is *medical*. Your child has a disorder in the brain instead of the liver, lungs, or heart. Just as with medical condition, troubled children are found in all types of families—regardless of income, education, race, or family history. Caring and loving parents are just as likely to have a very troubled child as are parents with a history of child abuse or addictions. Sadly, like other cruel diseases, anyone can become a victim of a brain disorder.

You are not a bad parent.

There is a myth that bad parenting, neglect, and abuse are the sole cause of emotional and mental disorders and addictions. This is simply not true and has been disproved through research. I've been polling local mental health agencies who treat troubled children and asking about "bad parents": how many are so dysfunctional, neglectful, or abusive that they irreparably harm their innocent child(ren)? The consistent answer is that only about 10% to 15% of families they see fit this description. That's a small percentage. The vast majority of all parents and caretakers of a troubled child or teen are good people who do whatever they can for their child. Destructive, hurtful parents are the exception. Instead of bad parenting, genetics plays an important role in mental and emotional disorders. Approximately 10% of the human population worldwide is born with chronic mental illness or substance addictions. If you believe you're in the "bad parent" category, and have done and said things that were abusive, you can heal the damage by changing your behavior. You can turn things around *regardless* of your situation. Your child is *not* destined for failure. All you need is to learn how to parent your child differently, and take care of yourself differently. This will make you a superior parent and wise person, with gifts that will enrich your life and others in the future. If you are reading this book, you are like most parents who care a lot about all their children, and do their best regardless of their circumstances, education, and financial means.

Your child's future is at stake.

Mental and emotional disorders in children are disabling. Five of the ten leading causes of disability in children or adults *worldwide* are psychiatric conditions, including depression, schizophrenia, and obsessive disorder. (Murray & Lopez, 1997) Mental and emotional disorders are deadly. The table below shows that annual mortality rates in children and young adults with mental disorders are higher than mortality rates for children with illnesses like cancer, leukemia, and diabetes.

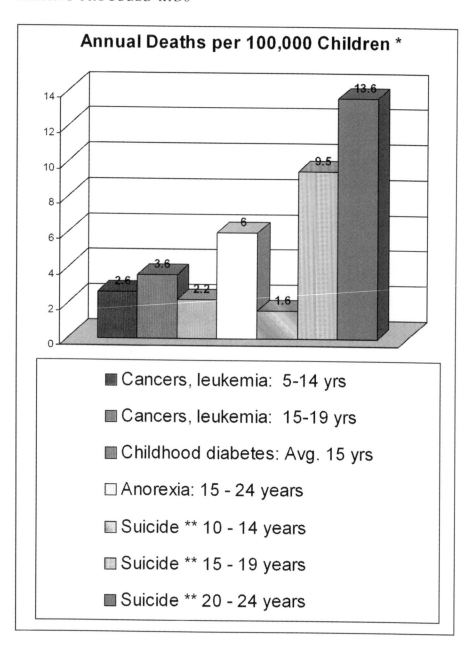

Annual Deaths per 100,000 Children *

- ■ Cancers, leukemia: 5-14 yrs
- ■ Cancers, leukemia: 15-19 yrs
- ■ Childhood diabetes: Avg. 15 yrs
- □ Anorexia: 15 - 24 years
- ■ Suicide ** 10 - 14 years
- ▥ Suicide ** 15 - 19 years
- ■ Suicide ** 20 - 24 years

*   Data is from the Center for Disease Control and Prevention, Atlanta GA, (www.cdcp.gov), and the National Institute for Mental Health, Washington DC (www.nimh.gov)

**   Suicides due to depression, bipolar disorder, schizophrenia, and other psychoses

You have every reason to want immediate, expert help for your child. Their erratic behavior is not due to "hormones" or a "phase," *it's in their brain.* Your child may face a lifetime of challenges because of a brain condition that is not his or her fault. You deserve the same compassion and support from your community as do other families with children who are sick with cancer or another serious illness.

Everything you've tried has failed.

Your troubled child is getting worse, and nothing seems to work. Despite your efforts 24 hours a day and 7 days a week, it's still not enough. There's little useful advice out there or explanations (even from doctors) to help you figure out what to do next. Families like yours face this all too often. There's not even place to take your child to keep them safe for a while so you can get relief and think things through. But I promise, you can learn new approaches and turn things around.

You need support, but you mostly get blame.

Families like yours also face the bad reputation or stigma attached to mental disorders. This is so unfair. If your child had any other major injury or illness, you and your child could expect to receive sympathy and support from those around you: prayers, the warmth of kindness, compassion, or even financial assistance from community fundraisers. This does not happen for families with a mentally ill child. Have you ever heard of a bake sale or charity event for a child with a mental illness or addiction? A majority of the population does not understand the scientific explanation for the behaviors of troubled and disturbed children, and it's common to blame these on poor parenting or weak character. You may feel that you are being judged by the very people you expect compassion from: close friends, family, doctors, teachers, and religious leaders.

Your troubled child has a true illness or disability, but people have a hard time believing this when he or she doesn't *look* disabled. Your child is not in a wheelchair or blind, they don't need surgery or a cast. Because people can't see a malfunctioning brain or feel the storms in the child's head, they jump to conclusions based on incorrect information and myths about addictions, abuse, or mental disorders.

Be watchful that you don't spend precious time or energy being resentful, defensive, or angry if others judge you out of ignorance. You don't have time or energy for this now. Focus on your important daily priorities and make regular contact with friends that are supportive.

Mental health treatments are disrespected.

Another form of stigma is criticism for the treatment you seek for your child. It is common for people to believe that therapists and psychiatrists are "flaky," or a waste of time and money. Some claim that if you see a mental health professional than you are weak, that you have a lack of faith or an inability to be strict enough with a child. Many believe that using medication is harmful to your child, and criticize you for drugging them to make your life easier, or to avoid your responsibilities as a parent. They are in the wrong, not you. These criticisms can cause you to feel doubt and shame at a time when you need support. You are not alone if you have experienced uninformed and hurtful opinions like this.

Don't face these challenges alone. <u>Find human kindness</u>; build a circle of support around you and the rest of your family. Seek out compassionate people and stay in touch with them. Seek those who are able to *just listen*, who don't judge, who sympathize and want to help but who don't try to fix all your problems. You may be surprised how many supportive people you have in your life that you haven't noticed before because they may not be among your present set of friends: a neighbor, the brother of a friend, the cashier at the grocery store, or a teacher at your child's school. They will offer a hug or a moment to listen or have words of hope from their own experiences.

ASSIGNMENT: Make a list of all those who have helped you in the past, and of those who care about what happens to you and your family.

೧౨

Most people find it rewarding to help another person who's been through some of the same problems. It is a natural human desire to pass along the gift of caring, to give back for what they received when they were struggling. When people offer to help, think of something specific to ask of them. Ask to meet for coffee, ask a friend to bring over a pizza, ask a friend if you can call to talk if you've had a particular bad day, ask a friend to bring over a funny film.

All families with disabled children have extra burdens. Your child is like other children with a serious disability or disease; you share the same challenges. They, too, must completely change their lives, but instead of therapy or family behavior work, they need special vans, or expensive wheelchairs or equipment, or special drugs and endless doctor visits and tests. They also make heartbreaking trips to the emergency room; they watch their child suffer, and they fret over enormous medical bills.

How can you cope with these extra burdens? Once you have regained the emotional well-being of your family, then you can think about getting involved in positive activities. Some parents have found that volunteering for mental health organizations has helped them in their own lives. Some renew their fun activities from gardening to reading to sports. *All* family members must go on with rewarding activities.

ASSIGNMENT: Make a list of all the things each family member is good at, including you, what they like best, and what situations they do well in. Then, help each family member enjoy their special activity within the next month if not sooner.

☙

There is hope, and you are the key. You can turn things around.

You and your family can be normal again. You can restore order and happiness to your home and you can once again become a safe, caring whole. While treatments are very important, you and your family have *the* most significant impact on the outcome of your troubled child, well into adulthood. Join other families who have taken hold of the reins of their lives. They cope better and take on a healthier attitude about daily struggles. They maintain safety in the home and handle crises better. The good news is that research shows that ongoing support for a troubled person results in a better long term outcome and future quality of life:

> *"Now, more than ever before, there is hope for young people with mental, emotional, and behavioral disorders. Most of the symptoms and distress associated with childhood and adolescent mental, emotional, and behavioral disorders can be alleviated with timely and appropriate treatment and supports."*
> —Federal Substance Abuse and Mental Health Administration.
> www.mentalhealth.samhsa.gov

Call it "X-treme parenting".

It's not about how well or poorly your child does, but how *you* cope with the situation and manage your family's life. Your parenting methods will not be like other parents. You cannot use common sense, or make rules that other families make to teach and control behavior. You will need to devise entirely new methods for yourself or get help from a class or therapist. You may need to reinvent everything you know from scratch, because each child and each family's situation are different. You will need to visualize a very different lifestyle outside of the norm.

Important fact: Punishments and rewards rarely work for a child or teen like yours because they can't think rationally, or they can't, or don't, think ahead about the consequences. Stop trying what's not working for you and do the Number One thing professionals do when they start to treat a troubled child's: praise good behavior (even the smallest things) and acknowledge each instance the moment that it occurs. This may not feel natural to you, but by doing it consistently, you will eventually see results. Another technique used by professionals is called "conscious ignoring;" they pretend to pay no attention to behaviors that aren't truly serious. It takes a lot of discipline and will power, especially when the child tries harder and harder to get attention, but I've witnessed therapists use this successfully because the child stopped! Gradually, you'll see problem behavior occur less and less, to the point where it becomes so rare that you forget the last time it happened.

In addition to encouraging good behavior, encourage your child's gifts.

> ASSIGNMENT: make a list of all the things your troubled child is good at, what they do best, and what situations they do well in, then set up as many opportunities for them to do these things as possible.

❦

Warning: turning things around takes all you've got.

Taking the reins of your household means everyone has to change, including you, and change is difficult. And there's a curious paradox: when you start to gain control over your child, their behavior gets much worse at first. Why? When a child feels they are losing power or control, they significantly ramp up their negative behavior before letting it go. (There is a psychological term for this phenomenon called "extinction burst.") In fact, you'll know you *are* making progress when this happens. Don't be surprised if other family members resist; they, too, are afraid of the uncertainty of change. You will need to stay strong through this difficult period, and you won't know how long it takes, *but it does end.*

❦

Behavior Problems 101

The reasons for behavioral disorders and addictions are still not well understood. How a brain functions and how it goes from health to illness and back is still on the frontier of science. The human brain is the last great unknown in human knowledge; it is an extraordinary and complex biological computer more advanced than our technological creations. If there is a "bug" in the brain's software or hardware, it can affect multiple brain areas, which makes it extremely difficult to troubleshoot. Even when a child gets professional help. it may still take years to understand and accurately diagnose what is really happening in their brain, and to fully treat all symptoms.

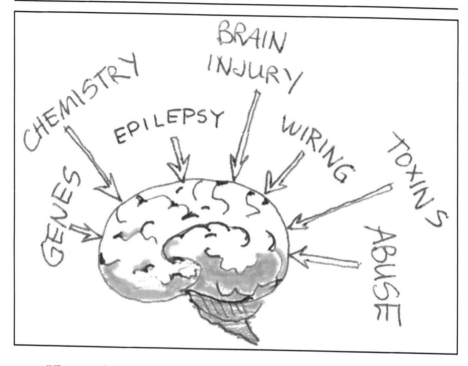

"Even when compared with diseases like cancer, brain disorders are notoriously complex. Scientists have only a limited understanding of the chemistry of consciousness, or of how problems in the brain's electrical circuitry affect the ability to form memories, learn or think."

—"Daring to Think Differently About Schizophrenia," Alex Berenson, *The New York Times*, Feb 24, 2008

Children are always changing because they are growing and their brains are still under construction, and each child's problem and path to healing must be custom-made to their unique brains and personalities. You will need patience. Treatment is a trial-and-error method that seems like a guessing game, but this is state-of-the-art in mental health, even for adults. But there is good news:

You can begin treatment and see improvement *without* first getting a diagnosis.

It is difficult to diagnose mental illness in children. Mental or emotional disorders are notoriously changeable in young people. The disease symptoms may be chronic, or may be a result of a current stress that goes away if something changes. It takes time to know which one it is. Many parents desperately want a diagnosis or an explanation why their child is having problems. But, quick answers aren't usually possible, and may not be that important. You should not ask "why?" but "how?" How do I work with my child? How can I be the best parent for this child and still nurture myself and the rest of my family?

Even the experts get it wrong

A child psychiatrist I know has a daughter with a mental disability, and he explains it took him about two years to establish a medication regime that worked for his child. He admitted he made mistakes, and once prescribed a medication "that was totally wrong for her." The doctor said, "I got a call from the principal's office the next day because she was screaming uncontrollably. It was embarrassing to be a child psychiatrist and go to the school and get my daughter who was out of control." After this incident, he sought another psychiatrist for her care, because he felt he was too close to objectively manage it himself.

> *"The psychiatric field is 50 years behind other medical disciplines, and child psychiatry is the youngest specialty in the field. It's truly an art until the research catches up and we understand the brain better. The more experience I have, the more I understand how little we know."*
> —Dr. Keith Cheng MD, Clinical Director, Trillium Family Services

There is no quick fix.

Brain recovery takes place s-l-o-w-l-y whether the person is being treated for an addiction, stroke, brain injury, or mental illness. You must accept that treatment may take years. For the majority of those with innate mental and emotional disorders, the brain never "recovers" per se, but the person manages the symptoms with therapy, self care, and medication, and they seem completely healed. People can know them for years and never know they have a brain disorder.

What can you expect for your child's future? It is best to look for gradual improvements, such as increased stability over time, but you should also expect a series of scary rocky periods that will test your mettle and faith. It will sometimes feel like your child is taking one step forward and two steps back. There will be periods where your child appears much better and fully recovered, and you are tempted to think the worst is behind all of you. But be careful not to relax or move into old routines or habits. Stay watchful and stay with your established structure in the home. Anything can happen: a stressful event, a series of nights without sleep, forgetting medications, stress at school... and your child's symptoms can worsen.

Recovery for one family's son

His psychosis in his freshman year in college came as a complete surprise to this stable loving family. He had all the classic traits of schizophrenia: he saw and heard things, he had odd fears and descriptions of events that went on around him. He was vulnerable to inappropriate people who took advantage of him. His formerly quiet calm mother became filled with anxiety and pain. In every word she spoke, her anxious tone seemed overblown to everyone around her; they thought she was the one with the problem. But she was lucky that her husband was always reassuring.

Over time, she and her husband supported their son as he went on trials of different drugs and drug combinations. They trusted him to take charge of his treatment. He learned how drugs affected him, and how the schizophrenia felt when it was coming on. He eventually found the right combination of medications with no side effects, and he committed to staying on them. After this period of about two years, he was able to finish college and get a job. Now he's happily married. His wife is aware of his condition and is supportive, and she gets guidance and support from her in-laws so she will be equipped and ready should her husband's schizophrenia emerge again.

CHAPTER 2
Take care of yourself first.

This chapter is for you. The task you face right now may require superhuman backbone and discipline, and saintly patience and forgiveness. The task you face is like running a 1000 mile marathon, then rowing across an ocean, then climbing a mountain. But you will start out stressed and exhausted. It's time to get in shape. No matter what, you must think of yourself first and set aside others' needs for a while. You must be as emotionally and physically healthy as possible to pull off this job of parenting a mentally or emotionally troubled child. You have no choice. Your troubled child can drag you and everyone else down along with themselves. I'd like you to stop and think for a moment about this question: How you are doing inside? Can you remember the last time you felt competent and capable and "fine?"

Admit that you might not be handling this well.

Ask yourself honestly about your own recent behavior. If you feel anxious and frustrated, even when there's no specific reason, or if you are very upset about little things, these are symptoms of your stress. In the ups and downs of normal everyday life, you would use your wisdom and experience to make the best of a situation, but your life isn't normal now and you are facing many more downs than ups. You are getting high doses of stress that make you feel and do things you would not ordinarily do. What are your symptoms? Over-the-top anger? One drink or two too many? Incessant nagging? Crying? Stress has built up for some time, and you probably don't realize how much it's affecting you and your loved ones. For the sake of your troubled child and family, **take a break**. You are not weak or a failure: you are overwhelmed. Go through the Stress Checklist below. These are the common reactions people have to high stress in their lives.

STRESS CHECKLIST

You feel sadness or blues that last for a long time

This is a sadness or heaviness that lingers for weeks and months. You may not even notice it anymore. You have memories of happier times, but you don't feel happy. You give up making plans for happy activities because nothing seems worth the effort, or because you *always* need to rest. You may not be aware how much you've become accustomed to these feelings. You may think you are a failure or weak inside, but this is depression. Depression is a normal response to stress and *not* weakness or failure. You will get your normal self back again.

What works to ease stress?

- Find someone who doesn't judge you, and call or visit when you've had a really bad day, and let out your feelings
- Ask friends for hugs or a joke
- Read a book that helps you escape your reality for a while
- Take a vacation, even if it's brief
- See a therapist for yourself, to learn ways to cope and feel better about yourself
- Consider the use of an antidepressant for 8 months to a year until your brain readjusts before considering tapering off

You lose or gain weight

Either you eat too much because it makes you feel better, or you can't eat because stress steals your appetite. If this is extreme in either direction (and you will know when this is so) please get help before the weight issue robs you of focusing on caring for yourself and family. If your weight change is not significant, consider dealing with it later, and don't "stress" over it. When your life improves, you will handle it like everything else, one step at a time.

You are irritable, even at small things

Do you experience a bit of road rage? Do you find yourself arguing with people a lot? Irritability creates a prickly atmosphere that stings everyone over time. It takes your focus away from your main task of creating stability in your life and it makes life hell for everyone else. You can stop being irritable. You must stop. Find something you can do that works to reduce irritability:

- Remove yourself from the situation once you realize you're in it. If you're driving, pull over and take a break. If you begin an argument, stop and explain that you're on edge, then take a walk. If you start feeling impatient, distract yourself with something else or talk yourself out of it: "I won't let this bother me; I can handle this calmly; I'm going to be OK…"

- Apologize once you've calmed down. Learn to apologize easily and quickly! You need not admit you "lost" an argument, but you can say you are sorry for your behavior. People argue all the time, but do it with respect and keep it short and always apologize if you get upset. Apologies are marvelous healers, and good examples for others.
- Count to twenty, ten is not enough. Take three deep breaths, one is not enough.

You are drinking excessively or using drugs; you are escaping through other addictions

Addictions are a very dangerous response to stress because they undermine you and rob your loved ones of your love and care. Take steps *now* to face and end an addiction because it poses an extremely high risk of loss to yourself and family! You don't have the luxury of making a few mistakes. Whether it's gambling, substance abuse, shopping, or sex addictions, you are hurting *everyone* around you.

- Take care of yourself *first* and seek professional help
- Find a support group for people like you who are trying to control their addiction
- Find information from a book or website about how to end an addiction

You can't sleep

Sleep loss robs your day: you react slowly, you forget, you make lots of mistakes. Losing sleep reduces brain function, and can eventually lead to physical and mental health problems for you. Sleep loss also leads to depression. Find treatments to help you to get regular deep sleep, for example: over-the-counter or prescribed medicine, an herbal tea, or reading (or being read to). If sleep loss is chronic, please get help from a doctor or try something called "sleep hygiene." Go to bed when you are tired, even if it's only a nap. If you wake up, frustrated, *trying* to sleep again, get up instead and find a quiet activity: check email, read, or do something useful with your hands. This relaxes you and helps you feel sleepy again.

You are forgetful, you feel "spacey"

Stress overworks the brain. It helps to reduce your workload, even if it's by a small amount. Ask yourself: what task or obligation can you drop for now to help you conserve energy? Think hard, because there are many more than you realize. Can you drop a responsibility that can be postponed? Do you really need to maintain something to perfection, whether it's a car, lawn, or hairstyle? Do you really need to answer *all* your email and phone calls? *If not critical, anything or anyone who takes your time without giving back should be postponed or dropped for later.* Remember, don't blame yourself or accept blame from another for not getting everything done. You have an excuse!

You get sick more often; you feel exhausted all the time

Stress weakens the immune system so people get physically sick more often and stay sick longer. Bolster your immune system, and stay physically healthy; it is essential for someone with your burdens! Take vitamins, drink lots of water, get exercise, and get sleep. Emotional and physical health are tied together, achieve one and you can achieve the other.

Demystifying stress

Scientists increasingly look at stress as an important factor in the origin of illness. According to a recent study in the *American Journal of Public Health*, civil servants in very stressful jobs are more prone to high blood pressure and heart disease. A divorce or a death in the family can weaken the immune system. Soldiers stressed by service in a war zone may suffer long-term physical effects, as has been documented in all major wars, from the Civil War to the Iraq War. Stress is not "all in the mind" nor is it a sign of weakness. Severe, prolonged physical and emotional stress has adverse physical effects.

UC Berkeley Wellness Newsletter 2006 (More information about stress is available at The American Psychological Association and the American Institute of Stress, www.stress.org .)

༄

You will continue to experience stress due to your child's needs, but it's how you *respond* to stress that matters most, because there are healthy ways and destructive ways. The following are actual examples of how stress harmed the parent's ability to deal effectively with their situation. You might consider how they could have responded differently, in a way that might have helped, rather than hurt, their situation:

Ben's daughter Sarah was diagnosed with conduct disorder, and she was very argumentative and accusing. Ben hated conflict, and he would do anything to keep things calm. When Sarah had raging episodes and kicked in a wall or broke things, Ben would repair the damage and go on as if nothing happened. Each time Sarah became dangerous, Ben's stress and anxiety grew, yet he kept everything inside. He felt that if he said anything—even calming words—it would set her off, and the conflict would overwhelm his capacity to keep an even temper. Even though he kept the peace, Ben stored resentment inside and got sick often. He spent so much energy avoiding conflict that he had no energy for the task of taking charge of Sarah's treatment and wellbeing. All his energy went into his armor.

Lisa's son Kevin would go through extreme mood swings over a few days: one day he could be overly energetic, and need 100% attention; the next day, he might hurt himself or attempt suicide. Lisa knew about bipolar disorder, but she gave up trying to help Kevin because "nothing's working." His needs exhausted and angered her, and she stayed angry. All she wanted was to escape her situation. She kicked Kevin out of the house and fought her husband John about the decision until John also left and moved into his own apartment. When friends asked her how she was doing, she'd say that Kevin was on the streets where he belonged and John was worthless, and her friends eventually drifted away.

Vera was an adult with Attention Deficit Hyperactivity Disorder (ADHD). She was aware of her ADHD and managed effectively her whole life. Her younger son Jess appeared to have inherited ADHD also. He was intelligent and creative, yet he was labeled a slow learner by his school. He had many friends, but was disruptive in the classroom. The stress of trying to help Jess with his school troubles stripped Vera of her normal capacity to cope with her own ADHD. She couldn't stay on track anymore. Her days were filled with feelings of guilt and anxiety, and all she could do was talk nonstop to anyone who would listen. Her friends tried to help, but Vera was stuck in a cycle of anxious behavior that caused her friends to avoid her. Her state of mind so completely overwhelmed her ability to work effectively with her son's teachers that they saw her as hysterical and out of control, which, of course, only worsened Vera's insecurity.

Make a list of your highest priorities

For you to make the extra effort to turning your lives around, you can't be drained by things that aren't absolutely necessary. Your problems are too numerous to solve all at once, so limit your energies to the highest priorities in your life:

1. **You**
2. **Your main support person or relationship**
3. **Your other family members, especially children**
4. **Your income and other basic necessities**
5. **Hope**

If you could get a total break from parenting and all other responsibilities for one week, what would you most want to do? What are some things you once enjoyed but haven't been able to do in a long time? Catching up on housework? Read a good book? Go on a vacation? A treat can be simple or grand. It's not selfish or self-indulgent, but like "medicine" for your own valuable mental health. A gift to yourself pays back 100 times its cost. You never know, but friends may want to help you relax and take a break. They've seen how hard it's been for you.

I know many parents who found creative ways to be good to themselves. One father bought himself a motorcycle. One mother allowed herself to indulge in chocolate once in a while. A single mother with two jobs gave herself permission to save up and purchase a pair of glamorous shoes. Some gifts to yourself might not be things, but time spent with others: take a son fishing, take a daughter on an overnight nature hike, go out with "the boys" or "the girls."

Next comes grieving

"I don't want this life anymore; I want what's behind Door Number 2."

— Mother of 15-year-old daughter recently diagnosed with bipolar disorder.

A sense of grief probably underlies everything in your life whether you are aware of it or not. Having a troubled child creates feelings of loss, like having a child with cancer. You see that your young person's mind and spirit are suffering, or you worry about their future. But, you also grieve for yourself. You feel robbed of a happy family life, good times, a sense of safety and security, time and money for enjoyment, and much more. And what really seems unfair, bad times seem to bring more bad times in unending waves of loss.

If you aren't feeling grief now, it will come. Grief will likely emerge as soon as your stress is lifted. In my case, grief descended like night, just minutes after I drove away from a psychiatric residential facility where I dropped off my child for the first time. Tears burst out uncontrollably. I had to pull over beside the road to let the deep sobs pass. I never saw it coming. One parent said she only got as far as her car in the parking lot of the hospital before sitting down on the asphalt and breaking down. Only moments before she was steady and strong and in charge of her child's intake papers with the staff. Siblings will also grieve, and they will start to exhibit their own behavior problems once they can let down their armor. *It is a curious psychological phenomenon that affects most people. We hold things together for a long time until it's safe to breakdown and release pent up feelings.*

Sooner or later, you will grieve. This is good. It's normal, and beneficial. As you go through this painful process you need the utmost in emotional support. Many parents have discovered ways to release their pain, and find inner emotional healing. I heard many examples that were different and creative, from parents who reported feeling better able to cope after they grieved.

A father found a way to overcome pain by chopping wood until he was exhausted; a single mother dug out a tree stump by hand to symbolically remove the deep rooted dead wood in her life; another mother went to visit a sister for a week and cried, laughed, ate chocolate, and talked till all hours: all she needed was to have her feelings acknowledged by someone who cared. Couples who were able to take a vacation alone together, even for a weekend, reported they felt a renewed bond between them, and they congratulated themselves for putting their relationship first. One parent held a simple ritual among friends in a forest, where she buried a poem about her pain for her daughter. Some people had the good fortune to find an accepting religious community or a circle of family members who would visit and sit with the family after a particularly bad day, or bring cookies, or play a card game.

Let grief happen. Until you go through the stages of grief (see list below), you will face each new loss as a painful reminder and you will revisit the same losses over and over again. Allow yourself to let go and move through grief so you can move on. There is hope. THIS WILL PASS. It may help to cry or to vent your anger or pain privately in a safe space like a journal. Once through your grief, you will be stronger and you will be able to see your life, your child, and your family with a deeper reservoir of energy and love.

∽

Grief has five recognizable stages that can occur in any order and be experienced more than once:

Denial
Anger
Bargaining
Depression
Acceptance.

Denial: or, "We don't have a problem, everything is fine."

Parents have a tendency to ignore, make excuses for, or find blame for problems brought on by a troubled child, and so can anyone close to the child. Some parents and family members are embarrassed by the child, or they are concerned about the outward appearance of seeming "nutty" to others, or "bad parents," or "out of control." They might also be getting accustomed to the behavior and think it will pass over time.

Are others telling you something you don't want to hear, don't understand, or that you refuse to believe? Do you have similar excuses?

"Stop telling us how to live our lives. Our son would never do anything like that."

"Nothing's wrong with my daughter; she is just doing this for attention."

"We can handle it ourselves with more vitamins and exercise. She doesn't need anything else."

"It's just a normal phase he is going through," or, "It's hormonal and he'll grow out of it."

"Doctors don't know anything. They just want to sell expensive drugs."

<u>Ways to deal with denial:</u>
Get information about what your child is like when you are not around. Ask others close to your child. If they trust you, *the* best source is your child's friends and peers! If you can, ask them if they have concerns about your child without making them feel like they are going to get him or her in trouble. Talk to teachers about what they observe of your child in school, *and listen carefully* to what they have to say—it may surprise you! Get second opinions about your child's situation from a school counselor, doctor, or therapist.

෴

Anger: "Stop this irrational behavior or you'll be punished!"

Are you angry about your situation, mad at your child or a spouse, mad at what people are telling you? Are you extra defensive, or easily hurt? Do you want to fight "the system?" OK, so something bad happened to you once and you'll never let it happen again; it's going stop here right now. You're putting your foot down, you're holding the line. But think: in what ways are you part of your problem; are you aggravating your problem?

> *In my experience, fighting often means that the parent and child really love each other, and really care about what each other thinks! Try stating this out loud and often— "I love you and I care about what you think."*

Face your demons. Look inside: we all have failings or weaknesses we don't want to face. We all want to avoid looking at our failings, and it's easy to explain it away or blame others. Face yourself honestly. Be clear about motives you don't like to admit. Are you worried about what others think? Will your social circle or co-workers push you away for being "nuts," "needy," or a "weak parent?" Are you afraid you can't handle your situation and will fail? In my situation, and this is embarrassing to admit, my child reminded me of other people in my life that I didn't like; I didn't realize until later that I was making my child "pay" for how I felt I was mistreated.

It's better to battle your inner demons before they spill out into your fragile family and your troubled child. Remember, you are not crazy or guilty or a bad parent, but are you possibly acting badly? Examine your life and think about how you want it to be. How will you feel about your parenting and your behavior once your child leaves your care? Reach deeply inside to find compassion for your troubled child, even when that child does or says things that are difficult to handle or hard to forgive. Mental disorders or addictions are often lifetime disabilities, and pitfalls for your child are around every corner. You may never be thanked for your efforts, but you will gain the peace of mind and courage you need to raise your very troubled child.

Some parents get therapy for themselves when they observe how their own behavior makes things worse; they learn to recognize what triggers them and how to manage their responses. However you choose to heal yourself inside, inner work will help renew your strength, so you can then set your child on course to a productive dignified life. You will never regret doing this important personal work, no matter how painful. The learning curve is steep, but inner work will make you very very strong.

You must be *better* behaved than other parents

You require extra self-discipline and inner strength despite your own stress and need for relief. Your troubled child might manipulate you, terrify you, push every button, and challenge every motive and belief you have. Under stress like this, even the strongest parent can lose the emotional stamina to control their temper or keep their cool, yet this is precisely when they must be strongest. If you can't catch yourself, *apologize* to your child and to others who are affected by you. If you look hard in the mirror and face your most embarrassing weaknesses, you are training yourself to be skilled at handling emotional nightmares with calmness and grace.

Ways to deal with anger:
Let your anger out in a safe place. Leave the room or go to your car. Vent your angry feelings to someone who can listen quietly and give you gentle feedback. Perhaps a therapist or best friend you trust who can remind you of your inner goodness. You deserve a lot of credit for coming this far and seeking help and

information. It's normal to be angry because of a terrible situation, but it's not OK to use that anger against others or yourself.

One mother's anger was extinguished quickly; she only needed a good two-hour gripe session with a friend. This mother let loose all the locked up feelings she'd saved for two years. Her friend did nothing but listen and express sympathy and concern: "I'm so sad to hear things are hard for you, and I worry about you." After this mother found understanding from another human being, she moved past her anger. You may need more than a single phone call, but find a way to release your anger and be at peace.

Your troubled child can bring out your worst traits and deepest fears, and you may not act appropriately. I bet you've screamed, eh? Screaming is very common, yet I've only see it bring shame and regret to the screamer. Forgive yourself; you've been stressed or frustrated, but screaming and emotional outbursts can hurt your troubled child as much as physical punishment. No matter how they react on the outside, they can't handle it inside. (Plenty of children grow up to be emotionally healthy and well-balanced after growing up in a screaming household, but a child with a problem in the brain can be seriously damaged by it.)

෨

Bargaining: 1) I will make sacrifices; 2) the universe will fix the problem; 3) mission accomplished.

I remember being in this stage, very proud that I wasn't in denial anymore and that my hard personal work cooled my anger and the inner pain it disguised. I was ready to make things right, once and for all, and through my hard work and sacrifice, I was going to beat all the odds and heal my child. It was a time of hope and strength—and it was a total fantasy. It can sound like this:

"We're getting a second mortgage and seeing the best doctors in town, no matter the cost."
"Lord, I promise to (go to church, donate to charity, stop drinking) if you heal my child and make this stop."
"His mother and I are getting back together for his sake."

"I'm going to use all my vacation days and spend a good long couple of weeks just focusing on her, and we'll turn this around."

Ways to deal with bargaining:
First, *there is no bargain*. You cannot make promises and expect a quick fix and a happy ending. There is no easy way out. You have hard work ahead, and you need to face your fears and do the very best you can. Hang in there, even if things aren't getting better.

๏

Depression: A sadness that never ends.

This is when you consider giving up. If you are in this stage, you know it's impossible to "cheer up" or think positive thoughts. Your brain won't allow you to, no matter how hard you try; all you can think about is sadness or heaviness and little else. You feel many losses profoundly: lost hopes and dreams, the cost of all the sacrifices adding up. You search for explanations. Have bad genetics sentenced your child to a lifetime of trouble? Was he or she exposed to something during pregnancy? Did I spank them too often? Was he or she abused by someone? The questions go around and around and until you give up. In this stage, some are tempted to escape these feelings by turning to drink or drugs, or they make risky choices for distraction. At its most serious, some parents consider suicide.

Ways to deal with depression:
Depression can be mild or serious. You can't avoid it, but you can ease your feelings and help yourself cope in this difficult stage. First look at your physical self: increased exercise is *proven* by research to relieve depression. Next, choose an activity that preoccupies you for long periods in a peaceful state such as gardening, cooking, or working with your hands. Then, seek things that are uplifting for you: be around people, read funny novels, watch comedies, listen to upbeat music.

When depression is so heavy that you struggle through your day, seek therapy or counseling, and consider getting an antidepressant medication. The combination of both treatments is also proven to be very effective for lifting depression. The clarity and ease you receive from medication can help you talk through the pain and learn to think differently about your life.

๏

Acceptance: Freedom from worry, healing, and strength.

This stage of grief is about being at peace with your situation, facing the truth without fear or pain. Having a centeredness and clarity about your loss also brings humility and wisdom, and a compassion for yourself and those around you. Accept your situation. Acceptance is key to becoming a great parent, who guides the family with discipline and love. With acceptance, you can reconnect with humanity, and see beyond yourself, and at last, take charge of your role as benevolent leader of the family. Once you reach this stage, you can have amazing revelations:

> "I finally see how my child is suffering and needs me for support."
> "At least my child is alive and has a chance. Others parents have not been so fortunate, and have lost their children to illness."
> "I've faced problems in the past and got through them; now I know and can handle something really serious and get back on my feet."
> "Thank goodness we are all doing OK considering how bad things have been."

A word of caution: You might go through the painful process of grief more than once! It is exasperating after all you've done to grow and be strong again. Take my word for it, the challenges will continue and they will get bigger. Expect it. With each step in your growth, you get a new, more difficult test. These tests are hard but you will make it, you will handle them, and you will surprise yourself. You will be a fantastic role model for the rest of your family and friends.

∽

Ingredients for inner strength: Patience, Courage, Discipline

Patience

It usually takes a long time to discover your child's problem, and it often takes a long time for your child to benefit from treatment. Mental and behavioral health treatment is different from medical treatment because the brain is so complex and different from other organs. Psychiatrists, psychologists, and therapists cannot use blood tests to reveal a diagnosis. Instead, skilled professionals observe behaviors as they occur over time, and they make small adjustments in medication and therapeutic techniques. It is a cautious approach that can be frustrating to you, and it requires saintly patience. Brains recover, but they recover v-e-r-y s-l-o-w-l-y.

> *"In their enthusiasm, people forgot that the human brain is the most complex object in the history of human inquiry, and it's not easy to see what's going wrong... For one thing, brains are as variable as personalities."*
> —Dr. Steven Hyman, Professor of Neurobiology, Harvard University (and former director of the National Institute of Health)

Even addicted brains recover slowly. Because of this, the group Alcoholics Anonymous has several slogans to help members stay patient with their own recovery. They are a form of inner cheerleading that are valuable for you too: "Easy Does It," "This Too Shall Pass," and most important, "One Day at a Time."

Remember, there is no quick fix. When a child's behavior and functioning is chronically stressful to you and others, it's natural for parents to aggressively seek a cause. Some parents want to get it fixed as soon as possible. Parents have been known to pressure teachers, doctors, and other care providers to make their child better immediately so they can get some relief.

> *"The parents I have the most trouble with want me to give their child more and more medications to fix them. They don't understand the limitations and side effects of over medicating. Is it OK for a kid to stare blankly and drool just so they'll be easier for the parents? I don't think so. Sometimes what's best for the child is not always best for the parents. I have to look at the whole picture of the child's life."*
> — Dr. Keith Cheng, Child Psychiatrist, Trillium Family Services, Portland, OR

Learn from the bad experiences of other anxious families who desperately wanted their child to improve fast and were willing to try anything.

Eric and Jesslyn had a single-minded desire to get their son Tyler back on track with his behavior and schoolwork. Over time, their focus on Tyler distracted them from their important role as caretakers and nurturers of the *entire* family, including their daughter Terry and each other. Tyler was the subject of every conversation. He became the center of family life, which robbed everyone of energy and attention for each other. Even if Tyler made improvements, the parents looked for the next problem to fix. It was lonely place in that household for their healthy daughter, Terry.

Martha mistrusted "corporate" goods and services, whether it was food, news broadcasts, lawn chemicals, or modern medicine. As a scientist, she knew she could do the research, to find a pure, natural, and gentle approach to even out the extreme moods of her teenage daughter Kelley. Martha tried numerous treatments, and if one experiment failed her expectations, Kelley had to endure another potentially risky trial. The high niacin dose in one such treatment gave Kelley such rapid heartbeats that she would panic, breathe too fast, and become woozy; the herbal formulation with implied antidepressant properties made Kelley unusually angry and agitated; the neurofeedback had no effect at all. Kelley hated undergoing each new "cure" and rebelled more and more, screaming and cursing her mother.

Some alternative medicines and practices have shown promise for improving mental wellness, but the use of alternatives in mental health is relatively new and research is limited. Only a few are *proven* treatments that can work for most people. Recent research suggests that combining mainstream medicine and alternative medicine eases multiple symptoms. For example: combining therapy and medication with dietary change, vitamins, herbal supplements, physical exercise, and acupuncture may be beneficial.

❧

Courage

There is a popular phrase that says "Growing old takes courage" or "Life takes courage." Families with a troubled child have more need for courage than most other families! Summon up the strength you need to do your job. Be the best parent and best person you can be while your child is in your care. This is your one chance. Trust me: you will want to look back on your life and know that you've done the best you could.

<u>Why a fearful parent needs courage:</u>
You may be afraid for your child, or *of* your child. You may fear you'll make them worse, or you fear confrontations, and physical violence. When you avoid asserting your authority and rules, this creates three potential problems:

1. Your child's illness will not get better on its own. The serious behaviors will become the norm because you aren't doing anything to enforce respect and rules.
2. Your child will learn to use extreme behavior to get their way, even into adulthood.
3. Your child believes this means you don't care about them. Your family believes you can't, or won't, protect them.

<u>Why a controlling parent needs courage:</u>
You may feel you don't need courage because you are in charge and in control. But, control is an illusion: no parent can control the future of any child whether healthy or not. Your child is no exception. It takes courage to let go. It takes courage to live without certainty. Focus your energy on self-discipline and on balancing family needs, without expecting specific results.

<u>Why a raging parent needs courage:</u>
Rage is a threat to a family's mental health; if you often feel rage, clean up your act! If you easily get angry at your child and want revenge or to teach them a lesson, it is not OK. If you easily get angry at a spouse, other children, co-workers, even commuter traffic, it is not OK. No excuses. Have the courage to accept that only you can change yourself. You can become the parent you really want to be: the parent with genuine love and compassion for all who depend on them. If you've "lost it" and carried your anger too far, don't assume everyone will forget it, have the courage to apologize, and say you're sorry. Do this every time you become enraged by something, and you will eventually be able to keep your anger in check. Your child and family will learn from your discipline, too, and do the same when they lose their temper.

If you are having a hard time controlling what you say and do, first admit to yourself that your emotions are a problem. In a journal or with a therapist, look at your weaknesses and notice how they burden your family and your troubled child. Next, take the responsibility to work on your weaknesses. You are in charge of yourself, and you *can* change yourself regardless of any anger problems you've had in the past. Parents who have suffered abuse as a child, or parents who have their own mental health problems can be excellent parents if they try. It's up to you.

෨

Discipline

Your discipline sets the tone. Your family will notice when you start controlling your emotions, and they will learn this critical skill from you. On some level, they will understand that you love them very much. They may not trust you right away or acknowledge your hard personal work, but they will remember it because it is powerful.

Stop using. You will bring everyone down by abusing alcohol or drugs even if you never raise your voice or lift a hand. Your loved ones will feel that you abandon them and betray them, and leave them to fend for themselves, and force them to take care of you when they can't, or shouldn't.

Stop running away. Like substance abuse, if you indulge in distractions, or escape your responsibilities by "checking out" of your family's life (to party, gamble, surf the web), they will get the sad message that you don't care.

Stop playing the victim. It's true that your child's mental health condition victimizes your whole family, but if you use your situation to get attention or sympathy from others, it will subtly pressure you to keep things in crisis. Being a victim is selfish parenting, it's about your needs and not your child's.

Stop making excuses. This is another way of running away from responsibility. Start making changes now, take the first step. The next steps get easier. Eventually, you will start running *towards* success.

Choose your battles. Are you battling your family? Are you in disputes with co-workers? Are you fighting with neighbors? These battles may be a diversion that keeps you from facing more difficult challenges brought on by your child. For your own mental health, and to keep stress levels low, make the choice *not* to fight some battles. There are problems out there, but you don't need to fix them now. Focus your energy on the highest priorities that help you and your family. Give everyone a break, especially yourself.

Are you battling your troubled child? Battles bring stress, and stress aggravates their brain function. Confront them *only* on critical issues, starting with safety, then respect for others and themselves. You can reduce conflict if you let your troubled child have something *their way* on occasion, for example, permission to wear weird clothing or stay up late. Ignore things that are temporary and not truly destructive.

Are you battling the world? There are many injustices out there, including those in the mental health and addiction treatment systems. You are not alone in feeling unfairly treated, mistreated, or neglected, but do you need to fight The System now? Tackle these huge issues later, if this is your passion.

Attitude is everything. It's unrealistic to think you can stay optimistic and sustain a positive outlook because you have such a tough job ahead. But you can have a good attitude, and know there are difficult days ahead, but that you will get through them. Remember: you can choose how to face troubled times: talk with close friends, exercise, laugh, and take time with your other loved ones. A favorite choice for me was treating myself to a bite of chocolate!

CHAPTER 3
Take care of the rest of your family

When your child is mentally ill, the whole family is caught in chaos and whipped around by your child's energy and needs. Your family is under stress, too, and they need to hear the same consoling messages as you. Each person close to a troubled child carries an emotional burden: siblings, primary relationships, close family members, caring friends, *and pets*. You all need each other to be well. You all need to be OK. Check in with each one and find out how they are doing. Are you aware of how they feel? Don't be surprised if you open up a flood of anger or sadness, just let it come and don't take anything personally. People start to feel better once their intense feelings and anger are released, and this helps them move on.

- **Tell them they are not alone.** Other family members go through what you go through, feeling sad, scared, guilty, helpless, anxious. Tell them you are all going to work together to get things back under control to become more like a "regular" family. Tell them you are behind them 100%.

- **Tell them it's not their fault**. Lots of people experience mental disorders or substance abuse. Like any other illness or condition, it can happen to anybody. It's also not the fault of the troubled child or teen. Tell them everyone is basically good inside.

- **Help them take care of themselves too**. Give them special time, or permission to get their own special time, and reward them for bearing up the best they can.

Strong families win. Research on "support networks" shows that families who stick together under stress, and care for and support each other, have a huge positive influence on the future of an emotionally or mentally disturbed child. If you don't have a traditional family around you, there are good people who can substitute for an aunt or uncle, a grandmother or grandfather, a mother or father.

Let everyone know you are a team. Tell your family that you are starting a new program to get things back under control. It will be music to their ears! They need your leadership. Together, with their help, make plans to handle problems before they occur, such as a crisis plan to prevent violence. Discuss what each person on the team can do to ensure safety, respect, and school attendance. Let everyone think of a way they can support each other. Working as team makes everyone strong. As Team Leader, part of your job includes cheerleading: "we are sticking together," "we are standing up for each other," "we are going to be safe."

Take back the game. Your troubled child is making the rules and your family is caught in a game no one can win. No one can follow the rules of a mentally ill child even if they try. The child's crazy behavior forces each person into a role that they can't escape. Family members believe it is easier to stick with established roles no matter how irrational. These roles offer a weird sort of stability because as long as everyone knows their role, days are predictable, and oddly, seem less stressful. Yet it's like a dance where the dance steps cause people to trip over each other and fall unless they stay constantly alert. This game or dance has been evolving in your family for a long time and all have gone along without realizing it.

Change your family's behavior to change your child's behavior. You have the power to change this dance by making your own rules. When your change the rules for yourself, your family is empowered to change too. When everyone gets on the same team, your troubled child starts to lose the power to control your lives.

Take care of your other children. They so easily go overlooked. Young and open, they are flexible and accepting—this is good news when the home environment is healthy, but unhealthy in a family under stress. Siblings start to learn behavior that works at home (sort of), but will not work in the rest of the world when they grow up. Siblings of a troubled child will struggle with personal and work relationships because they aren't in synch with others, which is what happens to children in other stress-filled families where someone is an alcoholic or drug user. Spare them a difficult life path and bad memories. Take extra care of them, because they will be connected to their troubled sibling for a lifetime. Don't neglect *anyone* who needs you for a troubled child who may not recover for years, if ever. Your healthy children should not sacrifice normal childhood experiences and opportunities because of their brother or sister. Show siblings they are loved and special on their own terms. Give them some relief; let them be children. Give them as normal an upbringing as possible.

Brother with older sister diagnosed with borderline personality disorder – *"She would ask me for a hug and I could tell by the way she hugged me if it was OK to be around her or if I needed to leave the house soon. I could just feel it."*

Sister with older sister diagnosed with schizoaffective disorder – *"I could have been a more devoted sister but it was too crazy. I escaped, I left in my mind. I wouldn't let anything bother me. I dropped compassion and pretended nothing happened, I tried to forget about my family."*

Oldest sister with sister diagnosed with bipolar disorder – *"All I did was try to get away when she blew out. Then I got jealous of all the time my parents spent on her and not the rest of us. Now I just let them handle it and I take my younger sisters away to protect them but they still hear the noise so I help them feel safe, but it's hard sometimes."*

Mother with 16-year-old daughter diagnosed with bipolar disorder – *"Our middle daughter was really worried about losing friends and being embarrassed when people found out her big sister was mentally ill. We talked with this and prepared her to lose some friendships, but deepen others. It was a way to validate her view of reality but also give her coping skills."*

Protect your other children from your stress
- Do not burden siblings with your responsibilities.
- Do not rely on them to be your confidants or companions.
- Do not argue with your spouse within any child's earshot.
- Allow opportunities for siblings to get away from your house and family..
- Encourage their friendships and encourage their connections to extended family.

When all family members know they are loved, they will be able to stand together with you and change the energy and power structure in your home—your troubled child will not be able to disturb the balance so easily.

How things are supposed to look

Your "support circle" should have lots of people in it, because of the seriousness of your child. Invite every member that "gets it" about your special situation to help hold your circle together: grandparent, uncle or aunt, sibling, cousin, close friends. It's OK to leave out family or friends who blame or judge.

When I began building my circle, I lost many old friends because they distanced themselves when they heard my story. It made me rewrite my requirements for friendship. One of my "requirements" was acceptance and trust; a friend was anyone who took the time to listen without judgment or advice, who reminded me of good things about myself, and who checked in on me once in a while. Traits of good friends also included what they would *not* do: not share my story with others, or give unwanted advice, or tell me my struggle was "good" for me.

ASSIGNMENT: Make a list of the traits you need supportive friends to have. Do these fit the people you spend the most time with?

A strong family creates and enforces an environment where bad behavior can be controlled, where the troubled child gets constant reminders and support to follow house rules and treat others and themselves with respect. If there's a crisis, The Circle sticks together and enfolds. When a family circle acts together, it can reduce bad behavior and reinforce good behavior. Each family member offers steady and constant reminders, praises good behavior, and deals consistently with bad behavior. Your child is outnumbered by family members that together assert respect and house rules. This is powerful. Remember, as you and your family become strong, your troubled child will fight it hard. Everyone will need to support each other a lot during this phase.

Couples must remember their relationship first, as stress can harm the most solid relationships. A couple may disagree about how to manage the child or about the high cost of care, or will blame each other for all the problems, or one will "check out" emotionally or physically and neglect the other caregiver and family. Families like yours have twice the separation and divorce rate than the general population. Coping with a troubled child will bring out any and all relationship issues that may have been manageable in normal circumstances. If your relationship was mostly healthy before this period of stress, then it must continue to be a priority for you. If relationship problems loom, get counseling, if not together then individually, or ask for help from supportive friends: prayers, cheerleading, or the opportunity to vent. Schedule couple-only time, and schedule time off where each parent takes a turn at managing the household, while the other takes a break.

Couples must stand by each other shoulder-to-shoulder and present a solid front as the family leaders. It is as important as putting yourself first. Your parenting trials should draw you closer together rather than pull you apart. What helps is to plan ahead for inevitable disagreements: first, list all the things you agree on, and focus your parenting in these areas as much as possible. Work out the disagreements later, behind the scenes. Your goal is to move forward in small steps. This will start to bring peace and calm in the household and in family interactions.

Couples can figure out what each is good at and have that person "own" that role. You will each need to set aside your personal feelings for the ultimate goal of sustaining your family's emotional well being.

One family's solution - Susan and her daughter, Pam, constantly had arguments about who-said-what, and their household was always tense. Pam seemed to have a better, calmer relationship with Jason, her mother's boyfriend. Jason asked Susan to let him try communicating with Pam, and see what happened. Susan resisted at first, she felt that her daughter Pam had "won" because she was "inserting" herself between Susan and Jason. Jason suggested that if he saw Susan slipping into a fight with her daughter, he would use a code phrase, like "hey, what are the plans for dinner?" That was Susan's cue to change course, step out of the situation (and save face), and let Jason take over.

If a relationship becomes abusive and violent (emotionally or physically), this seriously affects everyone's mental health. It may be better to separate, and endure the pain of breaking apart as the lesser of two evils. Remember, your family is special, and it needs to be led by the most responsible and compassionate person. This may be one or the other spouse, or another family member, or even a foster family. It is a terrible loss, but may be the only option that puts the children first and breaks a destructive dance. You will never regret doing what's best for your children. If your relationship ends, seek intensive care and don't wait! If you lose a relationship, it is even more important to take care of yourself for the greater good of your family. You can do it. Do your best to move on without further damage because the consequences can be so destructive. Don't let your family's story end badly.

Kathy and her husband Ed often had loud disagreements; it was their communication "style." They had a teenaged son, Jamie, who began to exhibit bizarre behaviors and say irrational things. Kathy and Ed's confusion about this just increased the number and intensity of their fights. In turn, their yelling drove Jamie into psychotic episodes where he would slash himself or become physically violent. Kathy felt helpless; she tried to get their younger daughter, Beth, to make Jamie to stop his crazy behavior because their father, Ed, refused. But Beth couldn't possibly handle her brother or her family's strife. She ran away to live with a friend. After Jamie attempted suicide, Kathy took him to the hospital and broke down and insisted "some welfare person" get him in a foster home because she couldn't take it anymore. Literally everything had fallen apart.

For single parents:

As a single parent during my family's worst period of stress, I offer you truckloads of compassion and support. You are a parent who must make so many sacrifices that you need superhuman strength simply to maintain—you are also at risk of burnout leading to everything from depression, physical illness, to substance abuse. In some cases, a good loving parent has lost custody of their children because they had a breakdown, leading to neglect of their children.

Seeking a peer love relationship at this time also has risks. Finding love can seem to be the very best thing for a single parent with a difficult child. It is natural to seek love and companionship, and someone with great emotional needs like you may starve for this. Yet this can make you vulnerable and cloud your thinking. It can be difficult to judge a love interest and know if they have the integrity, emotional maturity, and compassion needed for a safe loving relationship with you, and most important, for your special family with its unusual needs!

You need a mature person: an immature person can become uncomfortable with your child's behavior, and jealous of the extra time you spend with him or her. They may be really confused about the disorder and its special needs, or they may blame you for the child's behavior or pressure you to punish them inappropriately. A mature person will not have these traits. You need a compassionate person: A compassionate person will respect and accept your relationships with your children, and help care for them because it is the right thing to do. You need a safe person: Predators look for vulnerable people because they are easy to take advantage of, and you and your family has a giant flashing "V" for vulnerability over your heads. Predators take many forms, some only want physical relations, some just want a place to live, some are pedophiles, some are violent and controlling.

Avoid people that make you feel bad inside. Have you ever had a conversation with a friend and walked away feeling bad, but didn't know why? It's easy to assume most people are friends, especially people you've known and trusted for a long time, co-workers, church members, hang out buddies. But it may surprise you how uncomfortable they start to feel when you have troubles with parenting an ill child. Many families have sought fellowship and understanding from others and discovered, unhappily, that friends and community seem to turn their backs on them or tell them to "pull yourself up" and "face it". This, sadly, is very common. It may come down to them not knowing what to do or say. It may come down to stigma—the myth goes that if someone has a mental disorder and exhibits troubled behavior, the person and their family are "bad" people: weak, wackos, drug users, or abusive.

<u>If your friend hurts you, another is out there.</u>

A mom said she lost her best friend of 20 years because the friend got tired of her talking about her 10-year-old son and her feelings of loss. The friend told her to get over it, and stopped all contact. The mother was so hurt that she didn't trust anyone to be a friend anymore, and she isolated herself like so many other parents. Her only regular social connection became a support group for parents with developmentally-delayed adult children. "They don't understand what I'm going through, but they kind of do, and they are the only people I can talk to about my feelings anymore. I can't even talk to anyone at work."

<u>If your community hurts you, another community is out there.</u>

A couple had a 9-year-old son that regularly became uncontrollably violent. They were surprised to find that their church congregation of many years distanced itself after they sought solace from several church members. They hoped for sympathy and compassion. The couple noticed that if another church member faced a crisis (like a cancer diagnosis), that member would receive visits from the minister, or prayers would be said on their behalf. But, these parents were ignored or avoided on Sundays after the service. Once someone told them that they weren't praying enough, and that was why their son wasn't getting better. Another said it was God's punishment for a past sin (committed by someone in the family). These things hurt. This family left that church, and searched until they found another pastor who understood, and a church that supported them.

Avoid situations that make you feel bad. Avoid being in a physical or social circumstance that makes you feel bad or inadequate, even if it you think you should be able to handle it. Do whatever you can to stay positive and conserve your emotional energy. You never know when the next crisis may come. Protect your wellbeing from the seemingly innocent things that drag you down.

Change the station.

A father was helping a neighbor repair a car in his garage, and the radio was broadcasting a highly charged political call-in show. The father got really upset by the broadcast. He came home angry and without intending it, began yelling at his troubled son, who eventually kicked in a door and threatened to kill him during their subsequent fight.

Stop the newspaper.

A mother of a deeply depressed daughter couldn't help but read all the news articles about people's cruelty, stories about domestic violence, murders, or physical or sexual abuse against a child. She said she couldn't help being drawn to stories that fueled her fear for her daughter. The obsession with bad stories dragged the mother down, and the hypersensitive daughter picked up on her feelings of fear and desolation. Their home was a place that was haunted by the visions of a terrible crime that never happened.

Walk out of the depressing movie even though you paid for it.

Or, leave the social circle that's ignoring you. Without guilt, drop the charitable activity that needs more from you than you can possibly give.

༄

Laughter heals.

> *"Laughter might be the best medicine for transforming the faintest of glimmers of hope into an eternal spring, reveals research at Texas A&M University that shows humor may significantly increase a person's level of hope, says psychologist David H. Rosen.*

> *"The finding, he says, is important because it underscores how humor can be a legitimate strategy for relieving stress and maintaining a general sense of wellbeing while increasing a person's hope. Previous studies have found*

that as high as 94 percent of people deem lightheartedness as a necessary factor in dealing with difficulties associated with stressful life events, he says."David Rosen, Professor of Psychiatry and Behavioral Science

"Humor Heightens Hope" Texas A & M University, May 1, 2005

Pursue happiness. Make a list of activities that have made you and your family members happy in the past. Restore these activities into your lives and *schedule them on a regular basis.* Include in your list some activities that you or a family member would like to start, something wished for but put on hold because of the demands of your child. Some of the best activities are easy to do and free.

Funny movies, picnics, parties, hikes, shopping, parks, train rides, the beach, the mall, fishing, playgrounds, sports, dessert, playing music or singing together, artwork or crafts, upbeat music and dancing, card games, pillow fights, funny people in your life, comedy recordings, comic magazines and books, kittens, board games. Be creative. Be silly.

Privately enjoy the funny stories about your child. One day, we went around my family support group, and each person told a funny story about their troubled child. The room burst with loud, long, healing laughter. Some stories were hilarious. It helped everyone openly say things they thought but were too embarrassed to share. Parents will admit wanting to strangle their child, or giggle inappropriately when a child makes ridiculous claims. Parents will suppress a laugh when told about a grandiose scheme, or when they are the target of a meaningless threat. In this group, all had experienced situations where the child's behavior was really funny even though if didn't seem so at the time. All children say and do amusing things, and it's OK to laugh about them, just not in their presence. Below are some funny stories told by parents and siblings:

"I took her to the mall and she found a sweatshirt and held it up and said "This is for MEEEE!". It said "Drama Queen Academy," which was so perfectly her. We eventually started calling her "DQ" for short."

"On the permission form for the summer camp was a space for "other things we should know about your child," and I wrote in P.I.T.A. He didn't say

anything then, but later he asked what this meant and I told him: Pain In The Ass. I was so embarrassed."

"Sometimes my son says hilarious things without realizing what he's really saying, like: "Mom, you really need to get it together," or "Why is it always about you?"

"My son used to call me the most horrible things he could think of, and once he called me a slutty whore and I just laughed, and it only made him madder. I told him, "Gee, I'd sure be having a heck of a better time if it were true."

"Once he had this huge blow out and everyone was screaming. He was chasing his sisters who were screaming and then hid under their bed. I locked myself in the bathroom to call the crisis line in a safe place. The crisis line lady could hear all the screaming and said "I can't believe how calm you are," and I said "Hey lady, I'm on lots of antidepressants." So then he wanted to get to me, and he began kicking through the bathroom wall from his bedroom. When he broke through, he got totally jammed in the wall. The crisis lady heard him and asked if there was some way she could help, and I said, "It's OK now, he's stuck in the wall. We can just leave him there until he calms down."

"We sat for two hours trying to sooth my sister as she cried about her horrible life, and how no one would ever understand or care. It was major drama, and then she fell back into the chair and said "Ohhh, I am so bereft of mind!", and the word "bereft" was so ridiculous that we all burst out laughing and couldn't stop."

"I looked out the window and my sister was out in the yard trying to cut her hair with the hedge clippers, and she was having such a hard time getting her hair in the clippers at the same time as holding them to cut her hair that I had to laugh before I could yell at her to stop."

"Our daughter was going crazy trying to finish all her homework, and we were worried that the stress would make her start to cut herself again, so we did what the therapist said and asked her up front if she was thinking about

cutting herself and she yelled, "No! Leave me alone! I'm too BUSY to cut myself!"

"My daughter knows all about different disorders and thinks she has them all and blames everything on me. But once, she said she wanted to lose weight and then later admitted, "Well, I tried anorexia but I didn't have the self-control."

CHAPTER 4
Safety First

Your family situation is a *special case*, and you need to manage very differently than other parents. Your family needs industrial strength safety. Your priorities and rules should fit the seriousness of your child's behaviors. You will have safety rules that most people never think about. These will be inconvenient at first, but they will be part of your household when everyone sees how well they work. Start by getting a S.A.F.E. attitude:

Safety first - All are safe from fear, pain, or loss: family, friends, and pets.

Acceptance - All accept the way things are today and move forward from here.

Family balance - Everyone's needs are met equally: not too much for one, not too little for another.

Expectations that are realistic - The goal is one step at a time, one day at a time. There is no quick fix.

❧

S is for Safety First
A
F
E

First and foremost, your household should be a place of safety where all members can be physically and emotionally healthy. They must each be able to function in school and work. This means no violence including emotional or verbal violence: no screaming; no parental fighting in front of children; no cruelty to pets. Safety means: do not damage or steal property. Safety means: no bullying or teasing among siblings or between parents and children. Safety means: keep the environment calm: lower the volume on music or television; block upsetting or violent images from television, DVDs, or the Internet; make a home where everyone can be comfortable somewhere. Safety means locking up items you use every day such as knives, tools, household chemicals, prescription drugs, and alcohol. You can probably think of more. It is inconvenient to makes these changes, but they really help.

Make an emergency action plan with your family

Plan ahead for *when*, not if, things go wrong in the future. When a crisis occurs involving your child, each family member should know ahead of time what to do, and each should have an assigned role. They can be as simple as knowing who to call, to as complicated as protecting other family members or getting the child to the hospital. Talk with your spouse and other children so everyone can state what they feel comfortable with. Each person needs a role they can handle, and everyone must know that they will be backed up or supported by the rest of the family. This is your team, and everyone is in this together. Have a plan for home, and the workplace, and school. Creating an emergency plan shows everyone how seriously you take the safety of the entire team, and how important their feelings are. This can be tremendously reassuring.

Examples of Emergency Roles and Procedures:
- Who goes out and physically searches for a runaway? This person should be able to bring the child home safely without mutual endangerment, or know how to work with the police or community members.
- Who gets on the phone and calls key people for information or help? Who do they call, the police or a neighbor? Does your area have a crisis team for kids? Some do.
- Who should be appointed to communicate with the child? This might be a family member or friend that the troubled child likes or trusts more than the others.
- Can a sibling leave to stay at a friend's house until things cool down? Which house?
- Who should step in to break up a fight, and what *specifically* should they say or do each time to calm the situation? Believe it or not, the troubled child can often tell you what words work best and what words make things worse. Listen to them.
- How should a time-out work? Who counts to 10 to calm down? Who leaves the house and goes for a walk? Which room can someone run to to feel safe and be left alone for a while?
- What should teachers or co-workers do to help calm down a situation and get their classroom or office back to normal as quickly as possible?

Act quickly to reduce stress. The experiences of professionals and families over the years have shown that a rapid cooling down of emotions, and rapid reduction of stress hormones in the brain, creates long-term improvements in behavior. This is called "de-escalation." Regular de-escalation helps a troubled person bounce back from a crisis with quicker recovery. Following are examples of good safety plans from parents and siblings:

Safety in the workplace:

A 19-year-old daughter came into her mother's work place regularly and screamed at her, demanded money, and hurled accusations in front of the mother's co-workers. Sometimes she would be high, and the office workers became fearful. The mother spoke to her supervisor about a plan. It was agreed that if the daughter came in, someone would immediately call security, and everyone would leave the space except for one other co-worker. This person would stand in solidarity next to the mother and stay there in the event the daughter tried something violent. They would wait for security or the police to escort the daughter out. The next time this happened, the daughter was arrested and held for a few hours and released without charges. The daughter stopped the workplace visits.

Breaking up a fight:

A mother and teenaged daughter would often become entangled in a fight, and the daughter made dangerous threats. The parents agreed ahead of time that the father would be called when this happened, and talk with the daughter about her feelings, and listen but not try to resolve the fight. The he mother agreed to leave the room while the daughter was talking with the father; and the daughter agreed to do what her father said. The father came up with several clever "time out" procedures that ensured the daughter's safety but kept her and the mother apart for a long enough period to calm them down.

Sibling safety:

In another instance, a brother was allowed to go and stay at a particular friend's house when things got too hellish with his troubled brother at home. This was arranged ahead of time and the friend's parents agreed to the situation. The sibling would simply leave home anytime he needed. He would telephone home and report where he was, and the friend's parent would get on the line to verify. The friend's family was often given cookies or a home-delivered pizza in thanks for opening their home as a safety zone for the brother.

Safety means occasionally breaking personal rules of fairness and privacy

But, this only works if you have strict personal rules of ethics! Some families are put into extreme situations or emergencies that require violating their personal beliefs of democracy, privacy, or fairness. This happens most often with adolescents who, because they are older, are going to be more deceitful or secretive about dangerous plans. Consider secretly searching their room, blocking a bank account, blocking a website, reading a private diary or email, listening in on a phone call, and tracking cell phone records. The following measures were taken by parents to protect a troubled child:

- A mother searched a teenaged daughter's room for the phone number of her much older male friend whom the parents felt was risky, and she read the daughter's diary. The mother didn't tell the daughter, but she was able to call the man and warn him that she knew who he was, demanded he stay away, and warned she would report any further contact to authorities and his employer. He stayed away.

- A father programmed the family's computer to track and archive all email and messaging conversations so they could not be permanently deleted. He reviewed the messages daily to keep track of names in case there was a need to call police or to locate his daughter if she ran away.

- Parents searched a son's room, and backpack, and all personal belongings for drugs and weapons. They found drugs and drug paraphernalia, and were able to get their son assigned to drug treatment through the local juvenile department. This was the start of getting more help for him.

- A mother recruited a "spy network" with her son's friends' parents and with employees of businesses he regularly visited with friends (such as a skateboard shop near the school). She was able to keep track of his associates, several of whom were adults that were known to provide alcohol to youth. She shared these individuals' names with everyone, including the school, and asked that they be watched.

- A father took the "spy network" idea further and had contact cards made to give to people: police, teachers, roommates, and the child's friends. The father asked them to please call him if they spotted his teenaged daughter in certain places where she was forbidden to go. This hindered the daughter's access to street drugs, and greatly improved her progress in therapy.

In the case of teenaged children, things that seem to be unfair or a violation of privacy will cost you their trust if they find out, and trust is a very important asset. Without trust, you unintentionally encourage lying and secretiveness or retribution. Be very careful about breaking personal rules: use your highest sense of ethics, and never use your actions against your child! If you have already betrayed or overreacted in their eyes, it will be very difficult to earn their trust again.

⁊

S
A is for Acceptance – accept things as they are today and move forward from here
F
E

It takes a measure of personal growth and maturity to achieve acceptance. Some say they turn to spiritual support. Accept that your family has a tougher job than others. Accept the troubled child for who they are, regardless of their behavior. Drop the façade that you don't have problems, that you have everything under control. Accept that you may not be able to handle things, and then accept help. You have not failed, it is not your fault. Decent people will accept you and not judge you; instead, they will admire your courage and offer steady help because it is innately human to want to support someone in need. Accept that you may need to set aside some personal dreams until things improve. They will improve eventually.

Your home may be visited by care workers, police, or by friends who've come in a midnight crisis. It's better to let neighbors and/or co-workers know your child has a problem, that you love your child, and you are doing everything you can to help. Many people (sometimes those you don't consider close) will rally around someone who is honestly and valiantly facing their burden and putting their child and family first. Pick them carefully and they will come to your aid.

⁊

S
A
F is for Family Balance – not too much for one, not too little for another
E

Your well being, and the well being of your family should never be sacrificed to the demands of the troubled child. Parents who are earnestly trying to do the right thing for a child in great need make this common mistake. Sacrifice seems to make sense until one realizes that in the long term, you as a parent may be harming your primary relationship and your other children through neglect. You need your healthy, functioning family to support you, and they need you to nurture them.

What an out-of-balance family looks like:

The troubled child gets all the attention, and lives in the center of a storm; other family members swirl around a whirlpool of chaos. One person devotes all energy and attention to the child. Since the main caretaker is completely distracted by the child, the others try to make do, but they also hide what they feel and think. It requires so much energy to hold themselves together emotionally, that each one falls apart once in a while, and does something that hurts everyone. Someone is always trying to get away from the house or avoid responsibilities. Someone is always pretending there are no problems even when faced with glaring evidence. Someone is always rebelling against the caretaker because they believe they should protect the troubled child. Someone is the strong one, the one that quietly tries to "save" everyone with self sacrifice. None of these roles are healthy or fair, especially for children. In the out-of-balance family, there is no break or safety for anyone. Everyone is always saving up energy and maintaining their emotional armor for the next crisis or disappointment.

What an in-balance family looks like:

The person who does the main work of managing the troubled child gets help from each other member from time to time. No one runs away from the family if things fall apart; they stick around until things calm down, but then they get permission to have personal time afterwards. No one feels they need to protect the child from the family; this person is instead redirected to help the child when they are doing well, but step aside when the family must take some extreme measures to control dangerous behavior. Those who take on the most stress are allowed to take a break, and receive acknowledgment for their effort.

༄

S
A
F
E is for Expectations that are realistic

Adjust your expectations. You may be a good parent; you may work hard to raise your child, and of course you expect them to turn out OK. If they don't, will you be disappointed or feel like a failure? This is not a healthy mental or emotional place! Every achievement is a gift, and every set back might be "*normal*" for them. Your child may never be completely "OK" in the common sense of the word. They are who they are, and it's not their fault.

Ask yourself if *your* expectations are realistic for a child like yours. If you are striving 24/7 to help your child stay on track, consider that they may be incapable at this point in their lives. Remember that their minds have abnormal senses and feelings that you can not see. Watch that you don't impose unrealistically high expectations on them for behavior, school, work, social skills, or other aspects of life. Keep your outlook tied to their actual strengths and weaknesses (the things you observe every day), steer them towards their strengths and away from their weaknesses.

Reasonable treatment expectations for some disorders:

Almost always gets better with treatment:
ADHD, depression, and anxiety disorders (except serious obsessive compulsive disorder)

Likely to get better with treatment:
Bipolar disorder; personality disorders

Rarely gets better, but function improves with treatment:
Psychotic disorders (schizophrenia, schizoaffective disorder, and severe bipolar disorder), profound autism, mental retardation

Academic achievement can be delayed or unobtainable

Shawna saw Mikela's grades fall so dramatically in high school that the girl would not graduate with her peers. This was more upsetting to

Shawna because Mikela had been an honor student, but now didn't seem to care. Mikela was diagnosed with depression and anxiety disorder. Shawna didn't understand the implications, and she tried everything to stop her daughter from "throwing away her future," pressuring with discipline and threats that turned into daily fights. A friend of Shawna's, who had a developmentally delayed sibling, helped to change her perspective by asking: What if she really can't keep up? Must she graduate by a certain year? What are the other options? Shawna said it helped her to hear these questions. She backed off from criticism, and later she realized it marked the end of their combative relationship. Mikela dropped out of high school and took a job, and after a couple of years got her GED through a local community college. A couple years later, after Mikela had improved dramatically with treatment, she entered college and stayed up with all her studies.

Social maturity is delayed

Emotional and mental chaos are so distracting to a troubled child that they miss the social cues and graces that help them function with other people. In school, in a job, in a shared living situation, in a relationship, even in public, they may behave oddly, or immaturely, or disrespectfully. Many troubled children are highly intelligent, but still don't mature emotionally by the time they enter adulthood. This has nothing to do with their gifts or talents!

Laura was worried because her mildly schizophrenic daughter, Jessica, was a loner in high school. She never brought friends home, or went out for fun, or showed any interest in boys. Laura had religious beliefs that emphasized the importance of family, but Laura was afraid that Jessica might never get married and have children, and that her daughter would lead a lonely, empty life. Laura asked a psychiatrist about this, and was told that Jessica's behavior was typical for schizophrenics, because solitude seems to provide safety from a world that makes them anxious and paranoid. The doctor said, "Jessica is stable and doing really well for her condition. It may not be a bad thing if she ends up alone if she's happy and lives with dignity." This was hard for Laura to hear, but eventually she accepted that Jessica might not go through life the same as she had, *and it was going to be OK.*

Common sense is missing

Your child is not like normal children, and he or she may get into the same troubles or make the same mistakes over and over again. Expect this. Their brain has a glitch in its software or hardware. They seem unable to learn from their mistakes. Often, I've heard parents speak in astonishment and frustration that their child has no common sense, or their child is irrational. Yes, they are irrational; that's the mental disorder. Perhaps they will never get it, but they can be reminded and guided over a long time period and eventually become "trained" to avoid certain mistakes, or eventually they will learn. Below are some common traits that a troubled child may never seem to grow out of. Are any familiar to you?

- Does not show common sense or do what's in their best interest
- Does not have good instincts for self-preservation or for avoiding dangerous situations
- Has difficulty making friends with decent people; tends to make friends who are risky or dangerous
- Cannot participate consistently in any scheduled activity: school, part-time job, sports, lesson, chore, or club
- Cannot function in a team or group situation
- Does not learn through standard punishment or reward techniques
- Rarely shows character strengths (if at all): honesty, tolerance, respect for others and themselves, self-control
- Does not make plans they can realistically achieve, tends to hang on to fantasies
- Does not think decisions through to the consequences

Keeping your child safe and growing is a lot of extra work for you, but this is true of any family with a very disabled child or teen (with such conditions as cerebral palsy, severe allergies, blindness, or a weak immune system). Like them, it helps to stay as positive as possible, and do the best you can.

CHAPTER 5
Getting things under control ASAP

You need to be back in control, and so does your family and troubled child! It isn't easy, but it's important for the whole family's well being. If you can help your troubled child or adolescent now, they will be set with a lifetime pattern of self-care and cooperation with treatment. Then they can avoid dangerous substances, destructive people, and unsafe situations. You want to help them now, while they are still in your care, because self-defeating behavior patterns are easier to change in a young person than in adults. This is your chance to rise to the occasion, and do a superior job of parenting.

Don't trust your natural instincts. Most parents have good natural instincts for raising children. They have a natural love and a desire to see their child do well; they will teach them how to behave, and they will combine rewards and punishments so the child learns discipline. In an ordinary family, if a child or adolescent misbehaves, they are sent to their room, to a corner, or they are grounded, or privileges such as watching TV or using a cell phone are taken away. If the child or teen behaves, especially in difficult circumstances, they are rewarded with extra privileges, a gift or treat, and lots of praise. The reward/consequence approach alone *does not work* for a troubled child or adolescent, and it is common for parents to keep trying these techniques because that is what they know. Sticking to old disciplinary standards, even standards that worked well for years, can aggravate behaviors in a child with a mental or emotional disorder. And it will frustrate parents immeasurably.

Behavior is *managed*, never fully controlled. Your child may never be like "normal" children, so your goal is to manage your child's troubled behavior, and reduce the *symptoms*. Hopefully, he or she can learn to reduce and control their symptoms by themselves. Professionals (therapists, social workers, psychologists) treat a child by using "behavior management" techniques. Simply put, professionals dispassionately observe how a child responds to a variety of life experiences, and note what relieves them and what sets them off. They change the child's environment, or change their responses to the child, to encourage appropriate responses and limit bad reactions. It sounds simple and obvious, but it takes a lot of careful observation and patience.

To explain: when your child acts out, think what happened in the moments just before, then note how your child responded. *Pay attention only to the here-and-now.* Try not to assume what the behavior means or what they are thinking

or how it will affect their future. Instead, evaluate what actually happens in the moment and ask: how critical is this? Do I put in a lot of energy now or save some for more serious problems? This is an important concept. Ask yourself: is this a priority? Take things one step at a time and expend your energy on the one or two most serious behavior challenges. You will get to the rest later.

Looking at adolescence, for example, compare a "difficult" teenager with a "seriously troubled" teenager. ("Difficult" teens drive their parents crazy, but usually grow out of their problems. "Seriously troubled" teens have a pervasive pattern of negative responses to their world.) The former may have piercings and may smoke cigarettes or marijuana, which can be upsetting. A seriously troubled teen will go much further. Some burn themselves with matches or breathe aerosol varnish. The smoking and piercing are not an *immediate* safety issue, and are reversible. But self mutilation and aerosols are truly dangerous and demand immediate attention. What do you do when there's such dangerous behavior? Search the home completely and remove all things a child or teen might abuse, such as flammables and aerosol sprays. Then search again and again over time, in case the child brings home dangerous substances or materials and hides them. *You cannot be rational with a seriously troubled teen*; they do not respond to messages that their actions will hurt them or others.

Example – Roger, aged 17, cut designs on his arm with razors. He also dyed his hair, then cut it badly with shears. He wore dirty torn clothes, and refused to use deodorant. Grace, his mother had to decide which was worse, the cutting with razors or Roger's looks? It was the cutting with razors. She tried reverse psychology: she complained a lot to Roger about his looks. Since he often rebelled and did things to bother his mother, this technique worked! Roger continued butchering his hair and ripping his clothes, but he stopped carving designs on his arm with a razor. His rebelliousness was satisfied without the pain and infections from cutting. But Grace took additional precautions: she removed or hid all razors and box cutters from the house, and regularly searched Roger's room for dangerous objects when he wasn't there.

Some of these unusual steps have worked for parents of troubled children. They reduced stress, and they allowed the parents and child to readjust their relationships with each other. Better relationships meant better cooperation with behavior management.

- Allow a child or adolescent to talk to themselves or to voices if they aren't distressed.
- Let them voice grandiose fantastic plans without arguing with them. Then connect their plans to something in reality, the here-and-now, such as homework or a daily activity that may lead to goals they believe in.

- Allow unusual body movements or physical activity, hand waving, jumping in place, rocking, as these might be comforting to the child.
- Allow some weird clothing if it's basically inoffensive, if there is decent coverage, and it's clean.
- Allow your child to make art, write, or play music, and put few limits on their imagination. They may create something that makes you uncomfortable, so pay attention to what it means *to them*. Ask them to describe it, and listen for themes or patterns reflecting their feelings and beliefs. Then decide whether the expression is imaginative and communicates something important about their nature, or something disturbing that needs to be addressed. Then make a specific house rule against dangerous, cruel, inhumane, or self-destructive expressions.

Quick review of basic behavior management techniques:

1. Observe behavior in the here-and-now without emotions or judgment
2. Note things that cause serious behavior and limit these in their environment; note things that improve their behavior and increase these in their environment
3. There is no one right way, adjust your approach and be flexible
4. Do not expect a troubled child to change behavior on their own; prevent bad situations ahead of time by making changes in your life and home
5. Troubled children and adolescents thrive with consistency: keep every day the same, every task the same. Avoid changes that surprise them and bring on instability.

Remember: don't let "crazy" behavior or a lack of common sense surprise you. Their brains don't experience the world the same as most. Below are actual quotes from young people describing their inner experiences. After reading each one, think how you might change your home environment, or your communications to reduce the child's irrational thoughts or out-of-control feelings:

Anthony, aged 14, diagnosed with early onset schizoaffective disorder: *"It's like the stereo is on, and the TV is on, and the radio is on, and you're talking to me, and I'm trying to read a book, and I can't stop thinking about every single thing at the same time."*

Solution for Anthony: A psychiatrist recommended removing as many sensory experiences as possible from Anthony's surroundings: no sounds, little to no interaction except as necessary; physical distance (no touching even to comfort); and a quiet dark room to "hibernate". Juanita, Anthony's mother, was skeptical about the advice, but it worked. Anthony stayed in the dark attic room to himself and was content when he was there.

Laurel, age 13, cut herself regularly: *"I feel more calm because the sting feels good and distracts me."*

Solution used for Laurel: A therapist recommended that Laurel draw "cuts" on herself with a red pen instead of a knife, and also wear a rubber band on her wrist and snap it when she wanted to feel a sting.

Joyce, age 17, diagnosed with bipolar disorder: *"I'm ready to explode, I can do anything. I feel like I'm as powerful as the whole world and nothing can hurt me."* (She said this while in the car with her mother, who was driving her to see a doctor. Thirty minutes earlier, Joyce had climbed the roof of her house, torn out her braces, and jumped off.)

Solution for Joyce: Besides medication, she needed to have someone around at all times to keep her distracted or ensure her safety. Her single mother, Bonnie, occasionally got a neighbor or sister to be around the house when Bonnie was at work. But on those days when Joyce was home alone, Bonnie was frantic and fearful. Eventually, Bonnie got social service support for enrolling Joyce in an after-school program until she could pick her up after work. Bonnie's stress was relieved, which helped Joyce too. Bonnie spent every possible moment with Joyce when she was around, and Joyce eventually stopped the extreme behavior and began cooperating with treatment.

Brad, age 7, diagnosed with ADHD. *"Everyone is always yelling at me and they won't stop. I wish they'd stop; I can't stand it anymore and it makes me crazy."* (This young boy heard his parents' disciplinary words as yelling even though they used a soft gentle tone.)

Solution for Brad: Using advice from a book on ADHD, Brad's parents, Thad and Malinda, stopped disciplining by talking, and continually repeating their rules. When Brad started losing control, Thad would physically pick up Brad and move him to another room, or remove the objects around him that he was throwing or damaging. Picking Brad up actually calmed him down considerably. Thad and Malinda discovered that gentle touch of any kind also seemed to help, and that they could touch Brad when he started to overreact, thus preventing many full blown tantrums.

Carrie, age 15, was undiagnosed, but a mood or obsessive disorder was suspected: *"I have to wear these pants today because we're having a math test and I only do well when I'm wearing them, the other pants make me fail and there's no way I'm putting them on."* (The pants were quite dirty and her mother, June, wanted Carrie to wear clean clothes to school.)

Solution for Carrie: June negotiated with Carrie to set aside the pants except for the days when there was a test in math. June said that the pants would last longer if they were worn less often and kept laundered. Carrie agreed to this, and together, mother and daughter eliminated one item from their chronic conflict about clothes and neatness.

Interventions

To work on problems like these you will need to devise an "intervention." This is where you alter your communications or make physical changes to keep behavior stable and reduce stress. An intervention may not make common sense to you, yet it may work because it makes sense to your child's different brain. You will have to be creative and try different things. The following example is a creative intervention that a teen's parents came up with by really *listening* to what their son wanted, even though it wasn't logical.

Example – Eddie was 15. He kept turning up his stereo to full volume to play the loudest and most grating music imaginable. No amount of requests or threats prevented him from doing this at all times of day or night. Jack and Susan, Eddie's parents, hated the noise as well as the violent lyrics, and asked why he wouldn't respect their rules. Eddie explained that the loudness helped him concentrate by drowning out "weird feelings" in his brain. His parents did not accept his explanation, plus they worried that the music would make him violent. The noise issue became a serious source of conflict. Eventually, Susan considered that Eddie might be telling the truth. She got him a set of headphones so he could listen as loud as he wanted, whenever he wanted, and it wouldn't bother anyone else. And indeed, Jack and Susan observed that he was always reading or drawing quietly while listening through the headphones. There was no evidence of violence in either his choice of reading materials or in his drawings. Their music conflict ended.

Behavior management means listening and observing your child without assumptions or fears. Behavior management means you must distance yourself emotionally, and be quiet and calm inside. It means you must communicate simply, in a neutral tone of voice, because it helps reduce your child's stress, it keeps them stable, and it helps them listen. Spell out clearly what behavior you want from them (not what you don't want). If done well, you can help your child avoid dangerous and destructive activities—like this matter-of-fact parent did with her seriously depressed and anxious daughter:

> *"I'm going to the store now and I don't want you to hurt yourself or think about suicide, I'll be back at 11:30, and I want you to agree to stay here in your room, and not get any knives or scissors from the kitchen, and not think about hurting yourself. OK?" I can get you a treat; what would you like?"*
>
> — (The daughter calmly agreed not to hurt herself, and then she asked for corn chips.)

◠୨

What your child needs most for their future: INSIGHT + STABILITY + RESILIENCE

1. **Insight – self awareness**
   Insight allows a child to recognize they have a problem, and differentiate between what's real and what's not real, and how to act. Clear self-awareness allows them to respond appropriately to what's "real" and not chaotic messages in their brain. For those children who are able to learn this way (some disorders, sadly, prevent this), they can respond consciously and choose reality-based actions. Knowing and admitting they have a problem, and knowing they must do something about it is a very powerful skill once they become adults.

2. **Stability – fewer falls or softer falls**

Your child is like a boat that's easy to tip over; any little wave will capsize them, and everyday life is full of waves, big and small. Your job is to give them the skills to handle most of the waves most of the time. Mental health and addiction recovery professionals help children by training them to have certain traits and habits that help them cope with life's storms. It won't be as simple as counting to 10 to calm down, so work together with professionals by having the same training reinforced in the home. There is more later in this chapter about how to build stability in the home.

Your job is to notice when the troubled child is starting to struggle within, and anticipate what will be stressful, and seek ways to prevent or soften a crash, or calm them down when they start to spin out of control. You can then teach them how to do it on their own. For example, immediately remove the source of stress, or get them away from it. Then immediately do something else to ensure the stress doesn't come back: change the subject, distract them with another activity. Eventually, your child will learn, with your guidance, how to sense when trouble is coming on, avoid the thing that causes troubled feelings, and ask others for help. **Sense it. Avoid it. Ask for Help.**

3. **Resilience – bounce back when they fall**

Resilience is possible, but troubled children have a much harder time bouncing back. They can have extreme responses to simple disappointments like breaking a toy, or poor grades, or something as serious as the parents' divorce. Your goal is to guide and train your child to use their inner ability for recovering from life's many setbacks.

> *"…We are all born with an innate capacity for resilience, by which we are able to develop social competence, problem-solving skills, a critical consciousness, autonomy, and a sense of purpose." "Several research studies followed individuals over the course of a lifespan and consistently documented that between half and two-thirds of children growing up in families with mentally ill, alcoholic, abusive, or criminally involved parents, or in poverty-stricken or war-torn communities, do overcome the odds and turn a life trajectory of risk into one that manifests "resilience," the term used to describe a set of qualities that*

foster a process of successful adaptation and transformation despite risk and adversity..."
— *Fall 2007 e-newsletter, http://www.athealth.com*

❧

The magic of structure and boundaries. You will get back in control of your household when you have the focus, commitment, and endurance to change the way your house is run. Planned house activities and rules are called "structure." The concept is simple; structure is a set of expectations, rules, and schedules that everyone follows... *and it works!* Structure provides a safe, orderly, and secure environment for healing that is used in mental health, alcohol, and drug treatment programs for both adults and children.

Order on the outside helps keep order on the inside. Structure leads to a smooth flow in the home because everyone knows what to do and there are no surprises. There are lines that cannot be crossed by anyone (including you) and these are called "boundaries." Clear rules and expectations have a stabilizing influence on a troubled child's brain, but also help any family member under stress.

When a child or young person is distracted by uncontrollable thoughts or feelings, structure helps them track time and feel secure, and become more aware of others. It is a beneficial distraction. When each day can be kept the same as possible with a regular routine, the routine becomes a habit. This sameness has the effect of limiting uncontrolled thoughts or actions. It helps a child manage the chaos of thoughts and feelings in their head.

❧

Take charge

Parents need to be "benevolent dictators;" they should be completely in charge at all times, yet kindly and lovingly in the best interests of their children. **Your home is not a democracy.** You are the king or queen of your home; you do not need to explain or justify anything, nor get everyone's agreement. You, and only you, make the important decisions about safety and structure. It is easy to say this, but hard to do, unless you are deeply guided by love for your children. Your family will resist change at first, and you can expect your troubled child to put up the most resistance.

Note: this is <u>not</u> "Tough Love." Your goal is to enforce safety, reduce stress, and teach appropriate behavior. Your goal is <u>not</u> to punish your child, or allow them to go out and bring stressful consequences upon themselves. These only increase stress and reinforce their inner chaos. Instead, you can remove a privilege, assign an extra chore, or send them to wait somewhere and take time to think— "stand in the corner."

Troubled children and teens can be masters of manipulation. Chances are excellent that your child is already manipulating you in some way, and you don't realize it. Once parents figure this out, they're amazed at how the child knows exactly which buttons to push. In an instant, a manipulative child can make you feel guilty or anxious or angry, and get you to jump whether you want to or not. Why? Children like this have a heightened ability to sense to emotional cues. They keenly observe how you respond to their actions, which helps them use you to get things they think they want, or avoid things they don't like. Are they bad? Not necessarily. They are socially underdeveloped and powerless. Manipulation works for them because it gets, and keeps, their parents' attention.

Here is an example of manipulation that's hard to recognize. Let's say you want to teach your troubled child to have good character strengths. Like a good parent, you prefer to teach by example, by being trusting and honest yourself. If there's a conflict over their behavior, you clearly explain your reasons, you offer options to your child, and you negotiate an agreement that's fair and reasonable for everyone. In return, they are supposed to be considerate and reasonable too. But this does not work does it? Instead, you lose your authority and put your child in charge of the conflict. They do not understand good character. They only understand what they want and need this very moment, and they know how to distract you by using your own emotions against you. For them it's a *power struggle*, not a disagreement to be settled by reasoning and fairness.

> Elise, a depressed 14-year-old, began to have thoughts of suicide. As is common, she quietly began to dispose of her belongings and talk about life not being worth it, but her parents, Evan and Mary, didn't take this seriously. Elise wrote despairing poetry and made art with dark images, but her parents assumed this was just a phase. Her teacher noticed the red flags however, and the teacher informed Evan and Mary and the school counselor. Evan and Mary were very upset when counseling revealed the reality and severity of Elise's depression. They found a family therapist and gave Elise their total focus, they outwardly expressed love and caring to help Elise find meaning and joy in life. Their devotion worked until Elise turned 16, when the nature of her depression turned from inward pain to outward anger. She learned that if her parents made a rule that she didn't like, she could get dramatically upset and hint at suicide, and get them to back off the rule. Evan and Mary were caught in a terrible dilemma: Do we enforce our rules and get her so upset that she thinks about suicide? Or do we give in to keep her stable?

It is very tempting for parents to be manipulative, too, such as trying to control your child though lies, bribes, promises you won't keep, or threats. Eliminate manipulation as a tool in your home or it can create permanent distrust and anger, and worsen stress amongst everyone. The only time it might be OK to manipulate a child is when you are facing a crisis or emergency, and need to talk a child out of suicide or get them into a car to go to the hospital.

Expect backlash. As you become empowered as a parent, you become better at making and enforcing house rules, but you will get backlash from all sides. This backlash is a good thing. **Backlash is a sign that you are regaining authority and bringing order in the home.** Why? Your child and other family members each developed survival techniques or "coping skills" for living with stress and chaos, because chaos was the norm (the strange thing about these survival techniques is that they actually *encourage* the chaos). As you start making schedules and rules, everyone is forced to change ingrained habits and give up some of their control. It's hard to change habits, and family members feel very insecure when giving up control, so they will resist. See backlash as a good sign your work is paying off.

☙

What do the professionals do? In intensive residential psychiatric or addiction treatment programs for children is a round-the-clock team of staff working together with the child. Each hour is completely planned out and the routine is the same every day of the year. Each hour offers an opportunity to practice better behaviors and self control (medications support the ability to learn these). Rules are simple but strict, and the staff knows what everyone is doing at any given moment and where they should be. Many children do not like the restrictions and fight them at first, but eventually improve because the sameness and repeated messages steadies them, and the activities keep them busy and distracted from uncontrollable inner thoughts or feelings.

Structure: Sample Daily Schedule in a residential treatment facility

Time	Activity	Task *(monitored by staff)*
7:30 am	Wake-up	Change bed if needed, pick out clothes, shower, clean up bathroom
8:00 am	Breakfast	Wait patiently in line, clean up dishes
8:30 am	Brush teeth	
8:45 am	School	Special classroom rules and lessons
12 noon	Lunch	Wait patiently in line, clean up dishes
12.30 pm	Transition from school	Settle in room for 15 minutes
2:45 pm	Discussion group	Set a goal for the afternoon. Say one positive thing about the day or yourself.
3:15 pm	Snack, reading, or homework	
3:30 pm	If well-behaved: play.	If not well-behaved, write apologies or do extra chores
4:45 pm	Transition from play	Settle in room for 15 minutes. Wash hands when called out
5:00 pm	Dinner	When done, play outside or inside
5:15 pm	Settle	Go to room to play or read for 15 minutes, then quiet activity with others
6:45 pm	Group activity	Example: board games, art projects, movie, cooking projects
8:00 pm	Start bedtime phase	Brush teeth. One-on-one time with staff, read a story, make tea
8:30 pm	In bed	
9:00 pm	Lights out	

Rules for each task are written and updated on a white board that is posted visibly in a main room, with a line for each child and a specific chore or assignment for that day (such as laundry). Each task is checked off when it's accomplished, or if not, a consequence is assigned. The consequence is a task, such as pulling weeds in a well-defined area, cleaning three bathroom sinks, writing out an apology or a new goal for behavior. To promote focus and follow-through, it must be obvious to tell when the task is fully finished so that staff can enforce completion.

You can't possibly be on track and calm and alert for 24 hours a day and 7 days a week like in residential care! But note the concepts: Rules are very clear and very specific, they don't change, the child knows rules don't change, and any infractions are addressed by removing something fun and adding a chore. In the schedule, note that "transition" times are built right in. Troubled children need time to "change channels" to help them stay stable. Remember the goals: Lower stimulation = lower chaos = more stability.

༄

Four Rules for House Rules

1. Few
2. Simple
3. Fair
4. Strictly enforced

Despite your child or teen's irrationality, you should expect them to stay within simple rules—only the most seriously ill children will be unable to do this without intense treatment over a period of time.

Few
No more than three or four—easier to remember, easier to follow.

Simple
Think kindergarten. Make simple rules for ordinary things: chores, schedules, and certain communications. Write down the rules and post them, using very specific, concrete phrases like "Put your clothes in the closet," instead of "Pick up your clothes." Avoid rules where there is no clear way to tell if they are met. Use "Do your laundry every Tuesday," instead of, "Do your laundry once a week." Have clear rules about how to handle disputes. Instead of "No yelling" as a rule, use the phrase, "Both parties take a time out for 15 minutes if one starts to yell."

The rules below were developed and agreed upon by a mother and her 14-year-old daughter, and put on paper just this way and signed.

Daughter wants:
"Stop freaking me out and stop grabbing me when you want to talk. Notice the positive things I do instead of all the bad things. Give me a time out when I ask or when I'm tired. Don't stop me in the middle of something, let me finish first before I do a chore."

Mom wants:
"Keep the kitchen, bathroom, and living room neat. Clean up your mess right after you're done without being reminded. Stay and talk things over without storming out if we fight. Always do your homework after school."

Daughter promises:
"I will keep the bathroom, kitchen, and living room neat, and I will pick up my mess before starting something else. I will talk things out and not walk out on Mom when we fight, but I need to have a time out first and I need to take a walk."

Mom promises:
"I will not freak you out by grabbing you. I will point out the many good things you do and say. You can have a break after school, and do your homework later, after dinner. I won't bother you when you're in the middle of a project. I will let you go for a walk around the block, but I expect you to come back and talk if we have a fight."

Fair

Each family member follows the rules, including parents! If rules are fair then everyone is more likely follow them and they will encourage (or pressure) each other to do so. Most children and adolescents, troubled or not, have a powerful inner desire for fairness, and they are more likely to stick to rules if everyone else does and if everyone has the same workload.

Strictly enforced

Run a tight ship at home. You may be surprised how well this works for everyone. When I tried this, it was hard at first because everyone fought the constant limitations I placed. So it came as a surprise when, eventually, I got more respect the more I was in control. Your family members will be relieved even if they don't show it at first. The rules make everything easier and reduce anxiety. Use common sense and be flexible, set aside some rules temporarily if your child is in crisis or the family is too stressed that moment. Be very strict on only a few critical things, for example: have zero tolerance for dangerous substances and objects, unsafe people, and violence.

Joan spoke about her 16-year-old daughter, Alisa, diagnosed with bipolar disorder: *"She hated being grounded and was really horrible to me. But once she thanked me because she said she felt safe and was "glad because I know I can't do anything bad or get in trouble."*

∽

Physical safety

"I was told that I had to make Caleb's room safe, so I removed all his toys but that wasn't enough. He could still hurt himself on the furniture and bed or wreck them so I took everything out, and went and bought camping gear like sleeping pads, a sleeping bag, cushions. And that's all that's in there now. It's like his own padded cell and he likes it."

— Lara, Caleb's mother. Caleb is a 10-year-old with a type of explosive disorder.

Remember the "Safety First" concept in the last chapter? Remove, hide, or lock up dangerous objects and substances. If your child or adolescent has *ever* used something in a dangerous manner, remove the item even if they haven't done it since. If your child once held a match to a toy, you may have thought this was just curiosity, but looking at your child's overall behavior, don't take the risk of having matches where they can find them. Think: has your troubled child ever demonstrated an unusual interest in, or use of, anything dangerous? There are the obvious things like alcohol or weapons, but what about someone's prescription drugs, lighters, household chemicals, kitchen knives, power tools, or even tiny manicure scissors? It may not be possible to remove everything that might be dangerous, but definitely remove or secure all items that might be abused on impulse.

"I could tell my daughter was hallucinating when she ran into the kitchen. I followed her and she took the large kitchen knife off the magnetic holder above the stove and turned and threw it at me. It happened so fast! And it flew past me and stuck in a cutting board, and then I tackled her and held her on the floor. I took the knife holder down after that because I figured it wouldn't be so easy to get a knife if she hallucinated and had to search for one."

— Barb, mother of 14-year-old Katee.

Keep your home comfortable. Pay attention to temperature and noise levels in the home. Is it too cold, too hot, too noisy? Does your child complain about comfort things? Do everything you can to provide basic physical comfort. Even if you feel your child is just complaining and "should learn to live with minor inconveniences", your attitude may not work: not with *this* child and not *now*. You are trying to manage serious behavior. Physical comfort is important to their well being.

Guard valuable property. It's inconvenient, but if you have an older troubled child or teen, consider locking away money, credit cards, car keys, or easily saleable items like jewelry. Hide or protect anything you really care about that the trouble child might sabotage or misuse in some way. Even personal items of sentimental value like photos, collectibles, and books, can be destroyed as a way to get attention or take out anger.

Cleanliness and order helps. Keeping an orderly home is a challenge for many families, not just stressed ones like yours! Yet it is the very essence of structure and stability. Clean up or reduce visual clutter, do laundry regularly, clean the dishes regularly, have food in the refrigerator and pantry. If you cannot keep things in perfect order, maintain the best you can. Organizing is an excellent way to begin getting control of your lives. If it's impossible to manage an entire home or apartment, choose one important family setting that is kept clean and orderly. Make one space nice to be in: a kitchen, family room, or TV room. You will see your family enjoy this space, and you will too.

Repeat, repeat, repeat. Expect to repeat your house rules over and over again— many parents know this is common for normal children, but it is essential for abnormal ones! For them, external information is in the background as if they are in a bubble, and you must to repeat more often to get through. Not louder, just more often. Think of it as training a pet—you must repeat simple tasks over and over in simple words spoken calmly, saying things the same way every time. If your child doesn't seem to hear you, try something visual: post rules in several places, or use signs or pictures.

Schedule the same few things each day. Require that two or three things happen every single day at a specific time. Here are some ideas: have one meal together, do homework at 7 pm, read for 20 minutes, exercise for 15 minutes. Keep the agenda simple and you will get the rest of the family to buy in after a while. Place time limits on certain activities such as TV, or computer use, or gaming, if those activities reinforce bad behavior or limit healthier activities.

Sleep. Sleep is so critical for mental well being that it deserves special mention for two proven reasons: 1) mental health and clarity depend on enough sleep; 2) children with mental and emotional disorders tend to have disturbed and disrupted sleep schedules. Watch everyone's sleep patterns carefully, including your own. Remember how treatment programs planned their 24-hour treatment schedule? The child must be in bed at a certain time, and lights are out after 30 minutes. They may not fully sleep, but they are taught to remain safely in bed until such time as they adjust to the schedule.

Exercise. Brain health and physical health affect each other. You have heard these healthy life recommendations a thousand times, but I repeat it here because they also work for troubled children and brain disorders! Work with your child on each of these, one at a time:

- Eat normally or regularly
- Take care of your body, bathe or shower, wear clean clothes
- Reduce sugar and fats in food, take vitamins or eat vitamin-rich foods, drink lots of water, get physical exercise

"While researchers have long known that physical exercise can reduce the symptoms of depression in people who have milder forms of the disorder, additional research has been released recently that shows that exercise can also help people who have severe mental illnesses, such as schizophrenia, by reducing their psychotic symptoms. In addition to the mental health benefits of exercise, experts

are looking to exercise to help people with severe mental illnesses live longer, fuller lives. Due to lifestyle issues, people who have severe mental illnesses lose 15.4 years in life expectancy, according to the 1999 U.S. Surgeon General's report."

— *"Exercise Prescribed for People Who Have Severe Mental Illnesses", The New York Times, 12/8/05*

෴

Emotional safety

An appropriate emotional environment is one of the most important ways to reduce troubled behavior. Children like yours are extremely sensitive to the energies in emotions and the way words are spoken, both positive and negative. They can overreact or go from one extreme to another. The *sound* of negative words hurts. Professionals call this "expressed emotion"—it means that the tone, emphasis, and volume of a statement communicate more than the actual words and meaning. We know that family arguments are common so it may not be possible to stop all arguments and teasing, but you can stop it from reaching extremes and you can end the use of mean-spirited and hurtful words.

Positive expressed emotion can also be dangerous for some children (such as those with bipolar or ADHD symptoms) as it can pump them up too much. Watch out for wildly frantic play, or speech that may propel a child into dangerous behavior, such as trying to skateboard off a tall structure, or drink a dozen energy drinks in a row. You need to stop the extremes first, then work toward emotional evenness everyday. These are some things that are too intense and stressful for a troubled child:

Bullying and harassment - As quickly as possible, stop all teasing and harassment between *any* children whether the troubled child is the bully or the victim. Be alert, because it's easy for a stressed out parent to overlook subtle things (such as words spoken under a child's breath).

Physical fights - Immediately halt any fights that involve screaming or any form of violence, like kicking a door or throwing items. These are emergencies.

They may not seem serious now, but they can get worse over time. Fights like these can be stopped quickly, but only if the whole family works together as a team. First, have everyone choose a safe way to release anger, a "safety valve" away from others. Some ideas were mentioned earlier: go to another room; take a walk; sit and read; go to a friend's house; shoot hoops; check email, etc. In a fight, those who are most upset need to be encouraged to use their "safety valve" by everyone else in the family team. When everyone comes together to help all parties cool down, then its possible to talk about the issue that caused the fight.

Think up rules for "**fighting fair**" and teach them to your child or children. Put a time limit on disagreements, ban the use of foul language and name calling, prohibit personal attacks. Fighting fair is about disagreeing without attacking someone personally. In a fair fight, someone can opt out of the fight, walk away safely and end it without "losing" or being called a coward. The disagreement can be dealt with later when the parties have had time to think things through.

Mean-spirited language - *Words hurt a troubled child.* The old saying that "sticks and stones can break my bones but words can never hurt me" is NOT TRUE. A person with a brain disorder may repeatedly play the painful words they hear over and over in their head for decades. For example: use ordinary words to express how you feel, not to put down the other person. Right way: "This is a bummer." Wrong way: "This is f – cked, you a — hole." "Bummer" is low key and does not attack the person. It's normal that a family member can get upset and feel angry, but make a rule against using hurtful words and names.

Excessive activity and noise - What would bother you if you had a serious headache? A loud TV or video game? People running in and out? Loud voices? A dog constantly barking? Loud music? Sensory overloads like these help to push some troubled children over the edge.

Work on your own bad behavior! - You already know that you have limits and failings, and you need to face them. *Improve your behavior; it is your most powerful means for improving things at home.* It all starts and ends with you!

- Parents may not use put downs, complaints, or angry rants in front of children, no matter who it's directed at. You need to seem in control and powerful, and this makes you seem helpless. And this negative emotional energy worsens troubled behavior, no matter which person it comes from.

- Do not embarrass or criticize family members when you talk about them with others. If you need to vent frustration and anger about a family member, do it while away. Find a person who lets you say what you want, but will honor your privacy and keep it to themselves. Spare your family from your hostile emotions, even if they feel like legitimate emotions to you.

- Always apologize when you have misbehaved! This is difficult for parents but it gets easier over time.

- Do not use any children for your own emotional needs. Children are not therapists; this is a huge burden on a child, and it will affect them negatively in the future. Find an adult to talk to or to cry on a shoulder.

Pay attention to an unusual fear of someone - If your child gets unusually upset by someone, don't question the child's reaction or dismiss their concern. Allow the child to avoid the person's presence and don't challenge it. There may be no logical reason, but for the benefit of the child, you must stick with previous advice to reduce all stress. Their fear may be imaginary, but if it is not, it's serious. a *child's irrational fear of being with someone is a sign of some kind of abuse, verbal or physical.* Teasing, tickling, and bullying are abusive; sexual abuse is violence. You may be upset that a trusted loved one or friend could be an abuser of your child. It may not be true, but allow yourself the discomfort of wondering, and reflecting on past events. Take the time to think this possibility through and avoid pressing your child deeply for answers. It is common for abuse to be very hidden, especially sexual abuse, and perpetrated by someone you would normally not suspect. Get a second opinion from a therapist or someone else who works with difficult children.

You need to know everyone in your child's world. Who are the other children and adults they see regularly? How do they treat your child, and how does your child treat them? Depending on the person and the situation, a child like yours can easily be a victim of inappropriate words or deeds, or they will be inappropriate to someone else. Part of your job of being in charge includes being familiar with all the other people in your child's life, and building partnerships with the good ones.

Troubled friends

Get to know your child or teen's friends because they can have more influence on your child than you. Who is good for them and who is not? Troubled children and adolescents attract each other like magnets, and they attract troubled adults too. Troubled children seem to have an innate understanding of what each is going through and they comfort and affirm each other subtly or overtly. This may partly be a good thing, but they also reinforce risky behavior, model dysfunction, and generously offer danger. Your child could become a victim or a victimizer, or both, when around other troubled people.

I've found that parents often respond ineffectively to troubled friends. Some parents banish the friends completely; some ignore them; some welcome them to try and "be nice." None of these techniques quite work. To take and stay in control (as you should), have a plan for managing your child's contact with all people, and especially with troubled friends.

You are right to try to protect your child or teen from dangerous people at all times, but you cannot realistically block all contact. Before making a final decision about who your child is allowed to associate with, find out who your child is drawn to, and who your child attracts. Find out everything you can about your child's associates and know their life situations. You may need this information in the future to find a runaway or report to the police. When you understand the chemistry of their choices, then you can help your child reckon with situations that are risky, or you can better handle them yourself.

Case study: what would *you* do?

> *"He locked himself in the bathroom and refused to come out, and when I finally found the key and got in, he had crushed aspirin and was trying to snort it. It was only aspirin, but then I wondered how he got the idea about snorting it in the first place."*

Amy, the single mother of a 13-year-old named Chris, knew he hung out with a couple of 19-year-old men who weren't in school. Amy never thought about them before except to be glad Chris had friends at all—he usually didn't. She didn't know who they were or if they had jobs; Chris refused to tell her what they did together. Amy wondered whether Chris learned about snorting from them. Then she would doubt herself and question if she was just jumping to conclusions. Her head went around and around as she tried to figure out what to do.

- I want him to trust me, so I should trust him by not interfering with his visits with these friends, or maybe not.
- I'll ask him about his friends, but what if he lies? I know he'll lie.
- If he figures out I'm too interested in them, he'll be even more secretive.

- If I push for more details, he'll yell and scream and I've had enough of that for today, but…
- If I don't do anything about this I'm worried what will happen. Maybe it's nothing.
- What about these older guys? Why are they interested in my son?
- They wouldn't take me seriously if I talked to them. They might get mad. They know where we live and they could be dangerous.
- Once my son knows I'm worried, then he'll use my reaction to manipulate me like he does with everything else I worry about.
- I should do something, but I don't know what. Nothing else works. I'm so tired of this!

Has your troubled child ever caused worries like these, and you had nothing to go on? Even though Amy's gut feeling said something was wrong, her fear of facing her defiant son overwhelmed her with anxiety. What do you think you could do to handle a situation like this? *Hint: there is no one right answer for everyone.*

Protect yourself from false charges. Troubled children have told outrageous stories about their parents and others believed them. Often, someone who hears these stories decides to protect the child and "save" them from their supposedly "bad" parents. This can undermine a struggling parent's authority. Good parents have been mistakenly turned in for child abuse, perhaps for holding a child down so they wouldn't damage anything or run away. Good parents have faced the scrutiny of teachers or police officers or judges, and have had to tell their difficult story over and over again. Parents are humiliated when they have to expose their family troubles to so many people. It can attract more judgment upon you and your family and give you an undeserved reputation. Well meaning people can be ignorant of the consequences to you, if your child is lying.

Tell your family's story to important people in your life, their friends and friends' parents, teachers, and co-workers you trust. It could save you lots of grief from false charges.

Stop or defuse dangerous messages. Besides dangerous people, watch out for dangerous messages your child gets from the world. They may latch on to one or two ideas or beliefs and obsess over them. As an example, it's been common for media to subtly romanticize troubled behavior, drug use, and even suicide among celebrities and rock musicians. The implication is that crazy behavior makes one powerfully creative, connected, and rebellious. If your child feels crazy, they can be attracted to this message in music or video. A normal child may also be seduced by it, but is less likely to take it to extremes because they are better at weighing evidence and acting in their best interests. A troubled child can be constantly vulnerable to things they hear, no matter how irrational.

It may be impossible to keep the culture's dangerous messages away, but you can directly talk about them with your child, and point out the inconsistencies and fantasies behind the messages. Use your own memories of celebrities in your past; talk about the real world life of someone who was only "crazy" on stage. Talk about a celebrity you remember who went through treatment repeatedly, and had no career for many years, or who lost all their money.

Example of dangerous messages

A controversial anorexia website tells its readers that they can live without food. The site declares that food has toxins, that people who consume 1000 calories per day or less (a "starvation" diet), live longer and have fewer cancers and fewer serious chronic illnesses than the general population. For a child with an eating disorder, this irresponsible information affirms their desire for complete control over appetite. It justifies irrational thoughts about food, and gives them the confidence to stand strong against anyone's efforts to get them to eat normally. Starvation becomes their cause. A normal child may believe and follow the message for a while, but it doesn't go as far. They get hungry and move on. A child with anorexia-bulimia feels completely justified by this site's messages, and it encourages them to assertively resist treatment.

CHAPTER 6
Figuring out what's normal and what's not normal

L ots of normal children have bad behavior. But what's bad behavior and what's *abnormal* behavior? There are ways to tell the difference. Many children and teens have problems, even serious problems, and any child's bad behavior can be extreme and dangerous, *but they may not be abnormal.* The normal child or teen may genuinely be "going through a phase." What are some signs that your child's or teen's actions are early evidence of serious troubled behavior, the onset of mental illness, which calls for immediate attention?

Any troubled child can behave normally at times, and function well. Then they slip, and it's hard to tell how or why they slip. Is it a reaction to something that happened in the past? Is it diet or sugar, brain chemistry, or a learning disorder, or several of these? Patiently, you will tease out the subtleties of their behavior one by one, and help the treatment process move along more quickly. You must pay attention to little behaviors throughout the day and be honest about what you observe and not interpret what you see. It is very tempting to think that destructive behaviors are done on purpose to harm you or others, and to overlook the cause that something is wrong in their brain.

Some signs of *abnormal* unsafe behavior

- If they do something unsafe, it is not on impulse or an experiment but intentional and planned.
- They have a prior history of intentional unsafe activities.
- They have or seek the means to do unsafe activities.
- They have friends or others who are concerned or worried about your child. (e.g., your child's friend talks to you about this, your child's teacher calls).

൭

Researchers in behavioral and mental health have put together general descriptions to help people understand how a combination of behaviors (good and bad) suggests that a child will grow up normally, and how a different combination suggests the child will need significant emotional or mental health support in order to grow up safely and function in adulthood.

Behaviors at school

<u>Not serious</u>
> This child has occasional problems with a teacher or classmate that eventually are worked out, and usually don't happen again.

<u>Mildly serious</u>
> This child often disobeys school rules but doesn't harm anyone or property. Compared to their classmates, they are troublesome, but not unusually badly behaved. They are intelligent, but don't work hard enough to have better grades.

<u>Serious</u>
> This child disobeys rules repeatedly, or skips school, or is known to disobey rules outside of school. They stand out as having chronic behavior problems compared to other students and their grades are always poor.

<u>Very serious</u>
> This child cannot be in school. They cannot follow rules or function even in a special classroom, or they may threaten or hurt others or damage property. It is feared they will have a hopeless future, ending up in jail or having lifetime problems.

Of the four children described, the last two have behavior patterns that suggest they may never get the education they need to function in the world as an adult—they fall in the "abnormal" range. They both need help: the last one labeled "very serious" needs professional help and special schooling *immediately*.

Behaviors at home

<u>Not serious</u>
> This child is well behaved most of the time but has occasional problems, which are usually worked out.

<u>Mildly serious</u>
> This child has to be watched and reminded often, and needs pushing to follow rules or do chores or homework. They don't seem to learn their lessons and are endlessly frustrating.

Serious
> This child does not want to follow rules, even reasonable rules. They aren't able to take responsibility for their behavior, which can be aggressive like swearing and damage to the home, or passive like running away. They will do and say anything to get their way.

Very serious
> The stress caused by this child means the family cannot manage normally at home even if they work together. Running away, damaging property, threats of suicide or violence to others, and other behaviors require daily sacrifices from all.

Of the four children described, the last two have behaviors that suggest they may never have a stable living or work situation, which we all need to function as adults—they fall in the "abnormal" range. They both need help, the last one labeled "very serious" needs professional help *immediately*, and possibly medication and intensive mental health treatment to prevent damage or injury.

Behaviors in social settings, and with friends

Not serious
> The child has and keeps friends their own age, and has healthy friendships with people of different ages, such as with a grandparent or younger neighbor.

Mildly serious
> The child often aggravates others by arguing, teasing, bullying or other immature behaviors, and friends often avoid them. They are quick to have temper tantrums and childish responses to stress. Or, the child makes friends but loses them quickly.

Serious
> The child is frequently mean or angry to people and animals, and can be manipulative or threatening, or damage others' property. Or, they have poor judgment and take dangerous risks with themselves or others, and they choose friends who have dangerous behaviors.

Very serious
> The child's behavior is so aggressive verbally or physically that they are almost always overwhelming to be around. The behaviors are repeated and deliberate,

and can lead to verbal or physical violence against others. Or, the child spends all his or her time alone and avoids social contact as much as possible.

Of the four children described, the last two have behavior patterns that suggest they may never have normal adult interactions with people they work with or in personal relationships and friendships—they fall in the "abnormal" range. They both need help, the last one labeled "very serious" needs professional help *immediately*, such as therapy and mental health treatment.

These descriptions are *generalizations* and should not be used to predict your child's treatment needs; but they are useful examples of how professionals measure the severity or abnormality of a child's behaviors in different settings. If you are concerned that your child's behavior will affect their future, get help for them now. Early treatment while they are young and in your care works better than waiting until they've hit rock bottom as an adult!

Troubled kids switch between normal and abnormal. Your troubled child can be fine in one setting but monstrous in another—OK at school, but horrible at home, or vice versa. Many troubled children can hold themselves together for a period, but fall apart later from psychological exhaustion.

A troubled child has a disability, and it can be chronic, but the disability is psychological or emotional fragility. Their thoughts and feelings are more easily disturbed by life situations than those of a normal person's, who can learn to handle ups and downs of life easily.

ᝪᝯ

These things aggravate a fragile mind.

Overstimulation: A normal brain can easily filter out distractions such as sounds, smells, multiple activities or difficult thoughts or memories, but a fragile brain has a much harder time. When overstimulated, the fragile brain loses touch with what's going on—it might self destruct emotionally in a depressed child, or turn outward and take risks, break rules, or act on violent thoughts in a child with ADHD or bipolar disorder. **Make a list of what overstimulates your child and shield them as much as possible:** crowds, elevators, a dental exam, a sports event, crazy friends, everything in the house *turned on* (TV, stereo, video games, computer, radio, phones ringing, dog barking), family fighting or yelling, constant changes in places or people in their lives, etc.

Puberty, hormonal changes: Hormones affect all people, especially teens, but *especially* troubled teens. Some researchers suspect that hormonal changes may trigger the onset of mental disorders in young people.

Foods, fluids, toxins: Excessive sugar, alcohol, heavy metals like lead and mercury, caffeine, street drugs, and some herbal supplements, when used to excess, can affect a child's mental stability. Dehydration affects mood in many people, giving them headaches or making them cranky and constipated. A troubled child needs adequate water, and thus should avoid diuretic drinks (that stimulate heavy urination) such as energy drinks, tea, coffee, and caffeinated sodas. Some types of allergies will great affect mood and behavior for some disorders; a known one is wheat glutamine. Herbal supplements that are marketed for mood, sleep, and wakefulness, sleeplessness, for example, can negatively affect behavior or side effects with medications.

Boredom: Boredom brings on frustration and anxiety, a bad combination for a troubled child. To fight boredom, some parents try to involve their child in one activity or another, and each one leads to frustration and fights. Some parents allow their child to spend all their time on one activity that keeps them quiet and out of trouble, such as video games. (Many parents *depend* on the TV or video games to keep peace in their home!) But your child's brain needs to grow socially, emotionally, and academically. How can you prevent boredom, and help them grow, without exhausting yourself from the effort? Take one interest they have, and see if it can provide more complex experiences for your child and help them grow. This is a story about a father who turned his son's "mindless" video game obsession into an asset.

> Anthony was a 15-year-old with a long list of troubles with school and the law, and he had no friends. Anthony's conduct disorder had stunted his social development, and his emotional immaturity drove away all potential friends. He was regularly teased by classmates, which only made him act out in class, which then hurt his grades. Anthony escaped school anxiety by spending every moment alone playing video games. Anthony's father, Jerry, worried about the games' negative influence on Anthony, yet Jerry believed that his son might need this distraction to keep him from being bored and out of trouble. Without any opportunities to practice social skills, Anthony stopped connecting with everything but his gaming

box. Jerry met with his son's teachers, and together they decided that Anthony's social skills should be a priority. One teacher got an idea from her own teenaged son who was part of a computer gaming team. Teams had four players, usually other teenaged boys, who would enter gaming competitions. The players coordinated their actions to defeat other teams who were also part of the game. The teacher thought that team gaming would work for Anthony, because he could associate with peers who shared his interest. Jerry took Anthony to see a live tournament at a local gaming parlor, and enrolled him in a tournament class so Anthony could learn the rules of competition gaming. It was the perfect set-up and it worked. The rules, the structured environment, and the peer reinforcement helped Anthony keep control of his emotions and behavior. He made a few friends his age, and he adopted their disciplined approach to team play. Anthony's mood and behavior noticeably improved. For completing his homework on time, Jerry would also allow his son extra hours in the gaming parlor as an incentive.

Low sense of self-worth: Poor self esteem is debilitating on many levels. First, your troubled child is more likely to take out anger on themselves (self harm) or others. Or, they take risks or break rules easily because they don't care about the consequences. Your child might ask "Why bother?" if all they see are challenges ahead. Loss of self-esteem starves a child's resolve to take care of themselves and robs their hopes for a life with quality and dignity.

Harsh-sounding tones of voice: Remember that research has shown that troubled children respond more to the *sound* of a voice than to the meaning of the words, which is called "expressed emotion." Take a simple sentence: "Please feed the cat." It sounds OK at a moderate tone, but what if it's screamed: ***PLEASE FEED THE CAT!*** Harsh tones of voice are as painful as being struck.

Fear (for any reason): Whether it's genuine fear (such as a fear of being punished) or an irrational fear (such as getting germs by touching a door), fear can aggravate a child's fragile mind and set off troubled behaviors.

Abuse of any kind: Most people know that high levels of physical or emotional abuse can create emotional disturbance. Even milder irritations like persistent tickling or teasing can create high stress in a troubled child or teen. Pay attention that no one who is in contact with your child is abusive, as it can be easy to overlook abuse by family, friends, schoolmates, or acquaintances.

These things help a fragile mind

Absolutely clear, concrete, and specific messages: It is harder for a troubled child or teen to understand "Do your chores." To them, it's too general. The words offer no mental picture, or a clear beginning or an end. It is easier to understand: "Feed the cat and put your dirty clothes in the laundry bin." Be explicit every time, and calmly repeat yourself often. Some parents post signs as reminders, or post everyone's specific chores on the refrigerator.

Regular days, regular hours, 365 days per year, including holidays. Troubled children do better when their life is *predictable*, when the same things start and end at the same time, every day. This is not boring to them, but calming. Avoid changes in schedule or in routine activities in your home, and if possible, keep as many routines the same during school vacations and holidays. Many many troubled children and teens have problems during vacations and holidays because of the abrupt change from a predictable day (such as in school) to unpredictable and unstructured days.

Tiny steps to little goals. The child or teen does better with small achievable tasks like chores that can be completed in a day or less, or rules that require little effort to follow, such as avoiding specific swear words. Offer an incentive if the child can follow a rule for a day at first, then perhaps three days, then a week, and so forth.

A daily opportunity to do or experience something joyful. Art, music, physical activities, reading, or positive forms of play.

Praise

> *"He treats life like it's a musical, and he can break into song anytime and sing about anything that's going on, and it always rhymes. I told him he was really special, that bipolar disorder gave him extra talents and that there were many famous artists and other important people with bipolar disorder. Then he talked about it with the other kids at school and a couple of friends decided they wanted to have bipolar too!"*
> — *Mother of a 9-year-old diagnosed with bipolar disorder*

☙

Pay attention to STRENGTHS not weaknesses

The first task for specialists who train troubled children is to list the child or teen's strengths, then plan lessons where the child works within his or her best abilities. This helps build the child's self-esteem and encourages them to trust the trainer. One needs to be very observant and thoughtful to discern the strengths of troubled children or teens, and to creatively guide them to use their strengths in a positive way.

Strengths may not be obvious!

- Isabel is a moody and suicidal young woman, but her stubborn and willful streak is actually her strength. Stubbornness helps her persist with mood management and therapy. In her case, the trait is not a character flaw, but a potential life saver. She is too stubborn to give up on life.

- Micah is an 11-year-old boy with severe ADHD and violent acting out. But despite his condition, Micah has an ability to concentrate, and skillfully dismantle and reassemble appliances and electronics—the family's computer, their bicycles, the lawnmower, the hair dryer, etc. Micah's family tries to be understanding; they patiently wait until he reassembles important gadgets, like the printer. It is frustrating now, but Micah has a strength that can serve him well in a future career if he has a job as a mechanic or technician.

- Jeremy is 5 and has Fetal Alcohol Syndrome, which can seriously affect his future. His learning is slow, his social interactions always end up in fights, but his gentle, tender care of the classroom bunny is his strength. The bunny's food is always fresh, its cage always clean, its fur always brushed. This might help him support himself when he becomes an adult if he cares for animals at a kennel, a humane society, or a veterinary clinic.

Guide them to their gifts. After many years of listening to parents talk about their children, it's wonderful to hear how proud they are when describing their child's unique gifts and talents. Many think that the giftedness of those with mental disorders comes from their ability to think outside-the-box, or process thoughts faster.

- Powerful prose or poetry writing
- Excellent math, memory, or problem-solving skills
- Inventiveness and creativity
- Keen insight into people, and empathy for people
- Exceptional skills in art, athletics, crafts, or cooking
- Giftedness in performing or composing music

Many parents grieve as they watch their troubled child lose or misuse their gifts. The gift may not be lost or misused permanently, but it is hidden behind their child's disorder. It helps if you can provide ample opportunities for your child to develop their special skills: books of interest to your child, music or art lessons, or mind-boggling jigsaw or Sudoku puzzles. Remember: **many adults with your child's disorder have used their gifts and found success.**

> Adult man, aged 34, diagnosed with Asperger's Syndrome: *"I know this sounds weird, but I've had friends tell me they're jealous that I can focus so well, and in my crazy job, being able to concentrate really helps."*

> Mother of 18-year-old with schizophrenia: *"His paintings are incredible, they are like painted dreams filled with Jungian symbols and stories with lots of details. I hope he can keep it up because his art would be very popular. Everyone who sees them is fascinated."*

Good news from research

> *"Although individuals with serious mental illnesses are often unable to receive advanced education and find high-paying jobs, researchers found that many are able to overcome these boundaries. Nearly 500 individuals were surveyed who had been employed in professional, managerial, or technical positions for at least two years,*

and also suffered from a serious mental illnesses, including depression, bipolar disorder, and schizophrenia. They found that 83% had a college degree or higher, 62% had held the same position for over two years, 29% had held the same position for over five years, and 22% made more than $50,000 per year. At the time of the study 88% were taking psychotropic medication. When asked how they maintained their jobs, answers included taking breaks, medication, and support from a spouse, partner, or therapist."

— Ellison, Marsha L., Russinova, Zlatka. *A National Survey of Professionals and Managers with Psychiatric Conditions: A Portrait of Achievements and Challenges.* 2000. Boston University

A future based on gifts

Look far ahead. Adulthood is coming up FAST! Help your troubled child develop skills in something they're good at, and start now. Soon, they will have to manage on their own as an adult, and take care of life's needs: secure a place to live; pay bills; have transportation; interact socially in a reasonable manner; maintain their physical health and hygiene; and hold on to supportive relationships. If they can get a job, their chances of success increase dramatically. If they can't manage a job with a living wage, even a part time job is beneficial to their well-being and stability.

CHAPTER 7
Troubleshooting - Common challenges and how to face them

Problems with the mental health system: paperwork and people

The system for delivering mental health treatment is as complex and mysterious as the brain itself. A stressed out parent must go through a time-consuming and arduous maze of appointments, documents, authorizations, forms, specialists, agencies, and case managers. The last thing parents need is more stress, more time away from work, more questions, more insurance hassles, and a tighter schedule. Now *this* is insane!

<u>What helps</u>
Save *everything*. Save receipts, messages, copies of every form you fill out, even print out and save email. It doesn't matter if it's nicely organized in a binder or stuffed in a file folder or paper bag, just save it! Make copies of any document pertaining to your child including their birth certificate, social security card, and immunization history. Make a list of names and numbers of everyone involved with your child. Put these records in one place, so you can take it with you to meetings or refer to over the phone.

Problems with mental health providers

Too often, mental health professionals focus only on the child or teen. They may be devoted healers who care deeply about the children they treat, but they often miss or overlook the needs of the whole family. Family-centered treatment is complex and time consuming, and it requires much additional training. Many practitioners don't have experience with family work, and most do not have a troubled child. In my experience as a support group facilitator, I too often hear parents' stories of how a professional blamed or patronized a parent.

<u>What helps</u>
Insist on equal time for the rest of the family. All who are important in the child's or teen's life need healing and new sets of skills, and the first task is healing from stress. There should be opportunities for family members to meet with a doctor or therapist *without* the troubled child, to check-in and see how everyone is doing. This will start a conversation about how everyone can get their lives back to normal again.

Insist on being told what to expect. Another common experience parents have is not being told what to expect or why. You need to know everything they know, even if the professionals are still unclear about a diagnosis or treatment approach. Your child may have many physiological or psychological tests, expensive medications, or visits to many different kinds of 'ologists', and you may still not be clear on where the inquiry is going or what the doctors or therapists are looking for. Further, since they usually speak with or observe your child only during an appointment, they aren't fully aware of the types of situations that aggravate your child's behavior unless they ask you. **You are the expert on your child** and their behavior patterns; you are the expert on what drives them, *and on what drives them crazy.* Your insights are extremely valuable because you see the subtleties and patterns that are easily missed by a doctor, therapist, or school counselor.

Take control of the treatment. Ask to have one-on-one time with a treatment provider to describe your child's behavior if there are any changes, and ask them to explain everything to you. You are the customer and you have a right to ask for explanations. An experienced professional will listen to you, see you as an equal, and take the time to completely explain everything. If you don't think this is happening, consider looking for someone else. Like any professionals, some are competent, some are not.

Team up. It takes both you and the professional working together to comprehend your child's nature and arrive at a working diagnosis and treatment approach that works best. Develop a partnership and a shared vision with the professional so you can together do what's best for your child.

Are you being taken seriously?

True story - After a lengthy 2-hour session and a series of questions asked of both mother and teenaged son, the psychiatrist wrote: "the mother is over exaggerating her son's behavior. He can't possibly have all the symptoms she describes." The mother said, "I was completely ignored; this doctor affirmed [my son's] disrespect for me, in front of me, and [my son] got the idea I was full of it and didn't need to take his meds." She felt her authority had been undermined, and that she lost an opportunity to get her help for her son sooner. He was eventually diagnosed with schizophrenia, and hospitalized several times.

Unfortunately, this is common. I've heard many parents complain that doctors, therapists, or teachers don't listen to them, or parents feel subtly blamed for their child's problems. Researchers agree in an article titled "Uncharted Waters - The Experience of Parents of Young People with Mental Health Problems."

"Parents' distress is exacerbated by their need for expertise, but from those who don't take their concerns seriously."
— Harden, J, 2005. <u>Qualitative Health Research</u>, 15(2), 207-223.

I always appeared to be overly upset and stressed whenever I brought my child to an appointment because, leading up to any appointment, was a series of challenges and resistance that exhausted and frustrated me. It would have appeared to the psychiatrist, time and time again, that I was part of the problem.

"They see kids coming in when the family is at their worse, at wit's end because of all they've been through, and of course the parents' vulnerability stands out."
— *Mother of a 10-year-old with severe ADHD*

Problem - Blame, accusations, judgment

Few people are comfortable being around someone with bizarre or extreme behaviors. This is easy to understand. Parents like us can accept that others may not want to be around our child. After all, who else knows more about the stress they create? But it is most unacceptable and painful to hear blame or judgment from others about our parenting, about our child, or about our beliefs and character. Mental illness bears a stigma.

STIGMA: a mark of shame or discredit: **STAIN** <"he bore the *stigma* of cowardice">
Merriam Webster Dictionary

In historical times, abnormal behavior was blamed on mysterious outside forces that controlled a person (to speak prophecy, to succumb to evil spirits, to suffer punishment for past deeds). We now know from science about the brain and how brain function affects behavior, and about the roles of addictions, abuse, and genetics. But for some reason, our society now blames a child's misbehavior on character weaknesses of the child or family, or assumes the parents are abusing the child. This is simply not true for the majority of troubled children

I have yet to meet one family trying hard to care for a troubled child that has not felt blamed, judged, and accused by: best friends, close family members, a religious community, a co-worker, even medical and mental health providers. Nothing could be more wrong or more hurtful. Your child and your family should never have to face additional emotional burdens on top of what you already have.

What helps
Resist defending yourself; don't let other's ignorance bring you down. You may not be able to do anything about this now, you probably have no time or energy for correcting ignorance or hurtful attitudes. Consider avoiding judgmental people. Prune your life of negative things that take away your energy and create stress.

> A mother with a 17-year-old daughter asked for help in a support group: *"Can someone help me; I need someone to call my sister or mother and tell them that I and [my daughter] are not criminals or sickos. They've stopped calling, they refuse to have us over or visit for Thanksgiving and Christmas, and I just want someone else to tell them that she's fine now because she's taking meds, and that her behavior is OK now, and not her fault or my fault."*

It's common to stop seeing friends and avoid meeting new people. Isolation only makes things worse. You need as large as possible a network of compassionate people around you. If you think you can trust someone, **ask them to be your friend**. *You will be surprised how many people are out there who have a loved one with a mental or emotional disorder, and how many are willing to help because they completely understand what you're going through.*

You may find out who your real friends are, and they may not be family members or current friends. Real friends let you talk about feelings without judgment or advice, they are always around to listen, they help out with little things, go out for coffee, call to check in on you, or watch your other kids in a crisis. They may be people you never felt close to before but who have reached out to you with compassion. Accept their help, don't be too polite or too proud to accept the offer of support. Someday, after you have turned your family's life around, find another family who needs your support. Make a promise to help others in need, to give back to the universe.

Block unhealthy people from your life. There is a curious phenomenon where craziness seems to attract "crazy" people. They might be obsessed with a religious, medical, or philosophical belief and want to make your life their cause. If this happens to you, don't hesitate to end contact with anyone that wants to entangle themselves in your life and your child without your permission.

> Single mother with 15-year-old daughter: *"My brother decided I was abusing my daughter because that's what our mother did to us, and he said he was going to "break the chain of violence" and find a way to 'save' her from me. I found out from my daughter that he planned on "freeing" her so I got a restraining order against him. It was one of the hardest things I had to do."*

Problem – People who push alternative "cures"

Inappropriate advice has led many parents to chase cures and treatment that have never been proven to treat a serious behavioral disorder. Be careful who you ask for help or advice. Seek out people with actual experience, someone who has tried an alternative treatment or someone who has lived with a mentally ill or addicted relative who can tell you what has or has not worked for them. Some alternative treatments can help, but only trust an experienced practitioner with mental health care training.

<u>What helps</u>
> If someone pressures you to try some substance or treatment that *they* believe in, ask them if they've used it themselves, or have a loved one that was cured by this treatment.

> Parents of a 15-year-old daughter: *"People kept telling us about alternative treatments and we tried some, but then we found out some of these could actually hurt our daughter. The selenium pills someone suggested could be toxic, hypnotherapy could put her in a psychotic state because it had already happened to someone else with schizophrenia. The constant advice got so bad that the only way we could put off someone was to ask them if they knew of even one person with schizophrenia that was helped by this new treatment, and this stopped them [from bringing it up again]."*

Problem – Parents who complain about mildly difficult children

Parents of a child with serious behavioral disorders get tired of hearing others complain or gripe about mild behavior problems with their children. You know they should be grateful for their normal child! It might be very tempting to tell them to stop complaining.

<u>What helps</u>

Try just listening. Use this as an opportunity to show sympathy and understanding based on your own trials. It simply feels good to give back and help others. It will help them be more grateful for their children (as they should be) and learn from your strength. They will likely become a supportive friend instead of a complainer once they benefit from you wisdom. This has happened to me many times.

Problem - People who brag about their children

It's natural for parents to take pride in their children's achievements but many don't realize that sharing their great joy can increase your hurt. It's also frustrating to know that your child has great potential, or a giftedness that they can't express, which no one sees but you.

<u>What helps</u>

Whatever they are, share *your* joys too. There is no easy way to handle a proud parent without embarrassing him or her. Parents of troubled children interviewed for this book usually quietly bear boastful parents and their wonderful children. Yet you can be proactive and make a mental list of your child's gifts—*they all have gifts*—and stand on equal ground and share your joys. In my case, my child tested with unusually high math comprehension for her age. It was a source of pride I could share regardless of my child's condition.

Problem - Help is hours away

If you live in a remote area or far from mental health care services, your options may only be a family doctor, a school counselor, or a local clinic where no one has experience with a child like yours. Or, you spend your life on the road and your money on gas. If you only have access to local services, be extremely cautious with professionals who want to treat your child—they have credentials and licenses, but there are unfortunate stories of well-meaning professionals who mistakenly misdiagnose a child, and prescribe the wrong medication, because they were not trained or experienced.

<u>What helps</u>
Use ingenuity, resourcefulness, and emergency back-up plans. Each situation is so different, but these are examples of what some rural families do. Meet ahead of time with the local police or sheriffs to explain their situation, and ask them to help keep track of their son or daughter. Ask several friends to volunteer to be crisis helpers in case they need to drive a long distance for an emergency (e.g. watch the other children, cover a job position, or drive them if the parents think the child might get violent during the drive). Order medications through the mail (these are often less expensive too). Ask family or friends in the city where they take their child if they can stay overnight from time to time. Get a cell phone and an email account. Depending on the situation and the child's severity, some felt forced to take extreme actions, such as temporarily releasing their child into therapeutic foster care so the child can get regular treatment, or moving closer to a city.

Problem - the shocking cost of treatment

True story: Two parents sat in an emergency room at 1 am. They'd driven two hours to get there. They had no idea their son would attempt suicide; they never saw it coming. As they waited, they were asked to fill out forms and provide insurance information, but they didn't know if their insurance covered psychiatric care, nor how long their son would be in treatment, nor the costs. Because of the time, they couldn't check. They were told that their son needed to be held in the child psychiatric unit for at least a week. These were their choices: (1) take him home tonight and make phone calls during business hours next day to research costs, or (2) approve hospitalization and worry about the costs later. They chose hospitalization because of the severity of their son's mental condition. By day three, they finally reached the right person and discovered their insurance did not cover mental health care; by day five, their son started to be clear and alert from his medication. By day seven, he was ready for discharge. The week's charges were over $10,000, and the young man still needed ongoing psychiatric care and therapy. His parents drove him home with one week's worth of medication. And that was it.

<u>What helps</u>
Costs may be high, but planning for them is free. Before the $10,000 price tag happens to you, research financial resources ahead of time and look at all the angles. Start by looking at all expenses in your life. Examine your regular monthly bills in addition to occasionally luxuries; do you really need so many cable and cell services or magazines? Look at mental health treatment options, an experienced child psychotherapist might be more beneficial and cheaper than a PhD psychologist without child experience. A psychiatric mental health nurse practitioner (PMHNP) experienced with prescribing medications for children and adolescents is less expensive (and more experienced) than a psychiatrist who has only treated adults.

Do the math. These are things my family and other families have done to cover costs and help stay on our feet financially: purchased additional insurance; opened a "Medical IRA" account*; found public assistance (some is available for everyone, not just low income families); got a second mortgage they could afford; took on a second job; or postponed major expenditures (vacation, home improvement, car). NONE OF THIS IS EASY, but stable financial footing is critical to your family. Without it, how can you truly help your child?

* A Medical IRA account allows you to save for medical expenses and have all savings deducted from your income taxes, it's designed like a retirement IRA.

Problem - Very limited funding and support from schools

All school districts offer some form of education for "special needs" or disabled students, which includes children with serious emotional and mental disorders.

But many schools may not have specialized teachers for your unique child. Under the Americans With Disabilities Act, school districts are *required* by Federal law to offer precisely what your child needs to learn, yet many are not able to afford it or find it in your community. The lack of school support is very upsetting to parents, because they know their child must have an education to manage as an adult. Without an education, the child is at high risk of a poor quality of life in adulthood.

What helps
Search for different educational options. Rural or semi-rural residents must be creative: home schooling or boarding schools specifically for emotionally troubled children (see precautions below). Urban areas have more options: In addition to the above are therapeutic schools and day treatment, alternative schools (see precautions), residential programs with schools, or a GED program. Some troubled teens have been able to take part time courses in a community college or trade school in lieu of high school courses. It's always possible to delay school altogether, or to spread out course completion over time, even if your child is college bound. First, lower everyone's stress, then stabilize your child, then work on schooling.

A precaution about alternative schools:

Alternative schools that use an unstructured program where the child chooses what they want to learn may be better for your child's behavior but not necessarily for their education. Structure has been shown to help a troubled child the most. Alternative schools often attract other students with behavioral problems, who also can't manage a regular school setting. Putting chaotic kids together may really distract your child from learning! Look at the staff-student ratio, and ask if staff are trained in behavioral management. Visit the classroom often or volunteer if you can.

Boarding schools also need an extra hard look from you at their educational and behavioral approach, and staff qualifications for teaching troubled students. What is the staff to student ratio? Do they have licensed mental health specialists on staff? Do they have well-staffed activities and after school programs? Do they have a safe, structured living situation? A boarding school for a troubled child or teen should somewhat look like psychiatric residential care. Many boarding schools promise to make your child behave better and do well in school, but ask them *how* (Wilderness therapy? Boot camp? Strict discipline and punishment? Intensive religious immersion?). Some of these do not work for troubled children and can actually make things worse. Mistrust promises that seem too good to be true. See if the school can provide you with names of other parents who can testify to the school's benefits.

CHAPTER 8
Light at the End of the Tunnel

A ll we want is a good ending for our child. We want them to get better, and we want our life to be easier. But you will struggle with doubts. You will have times when it seems the problems with your son or daughter will go on forever. You will wonder if you can ever sit back and watch your child succeed, and if you'll ever earn that parenting award for a job well done. Now seriously, this isn't realistic for "normal" children! If you've reached peace of mind and handled things with grace, if you've changed your expectations to fit reality, if you and other family members start to thrive, if you've regained control of your life and persisted with self-care, then you DO deserve an award!

No one with experience in mental health can promise recovery, though many recover completely. Some children get it together in early adulthood, providing joy and relief to their ecstatic family! Some go through terrible hardships for years before they decide to seek help and commit to their treatment. I've been taking a straw poll for many years and asking a question of mental health professionals, parents and siblings of adult children, and adults with a mental disorder: At what age did you/your loved one start to turn life around and make the commitment to mental health treatment? The age given most often fell between the late 20's and early 30's. My own child made that miraculous turning point at 26. Will it be permanent? I don't know; I can only strive to stay a constant source of support and love, and go with the flow.

∽

The odds are good for living normally, or at least decently, with a serious disability when the person has support from a team of others. Below is a spectrum of outcomes that was developed by Dr. E. Fuller Torrey, an expert on schizophrenia, from his book "Surviving Schizophrenia." It is also applicable to other disorders.

1. High functioning
   Your child seeks treatment, stays in treatment, and maintains a functional life with positive relationships and employment. No one suspects they have a mental disorder.

2. Functioning
   With support, your child gets treatment, maintains good relationships, and has a job, but needs help if they break down in stressful life situations. With discipline, they stay in recovery.

3. Just functioning
   Your child functions, but requires regular medical, social, and financial support from others. They have a decent, safe life, but cannot sustain recovery or function on their own without help

4. Not functioning
   Your child barely manages even with daily support. They rarely work or avoid life's pitfalls. Your goal: keep them safe and off the streets, maintain a supportive, positive relationship.

Only time can give you a picture of your child's future, but I can give you a picture of *your* future.
   • You will get your life back
   • You will take the challenges with your child in stride
   • You will find joyous moments with them

- You will become wise and patient with everything else in your life, and others will notice
- You will have a strength that can heal others around you

Good people will admire you and seek your friendship and offer to help you. You will get back to the place you were meant to be, but perhaps a few years later than you expected. You will enjoy life more, *more!* You will gain great pride in your accomplishment as a parent who rose to the occasion and achieved a mastery that few parents reach.

∞

The following are true stories of families who moved forward with their child and saw improved behavior. They paint a picture of how the parent reclaimed their life and peace of mind. Most of these stories are recent and the child is still in the home, so there is no clear and final outcome. I hope these stories generate ideas for you for how to handle your own situation. Take the concept and experiment with solutions.

An overwhelmed single parent, Jim and his son Jake

Jim's wife abandoned him and their son, Jake, years before when the child was one. Jim stayed single and became a patient and steady father to his 8-year-old son, but Jake's explosive tantrums demanded so much from his father that it threatened Jim's job. Jake was 7 when Jim sought treatment because even he, a grown man, could not physically handle Jake without being hurt himself. Jim's employer became impatient with Jim for constantly leaving work, often once a day, to get a violent Jake from his "special needs" school. The employer had already accommodated Jim by allowing him to work after-hours and on weekends to catch up. They even provided a Jim a cell phone and truck. Jake had an excellent therapist with experience with explosive children, and some medication to calm him down, but progress was much too slow to ease Jim's work obligations. Jim worried constantly and never slept well.

Jim eventually met other parents, including single parents like himself, at a gathering at Jake's school. He stood around and listened to their stories, and he picked up useful information about the Medical Leave Act, about social support agencies that offer respite care, and about the use of "quiet rooms" for children like Jake. Jim cleared out a large closet and converted it into an empty carpet-lined room with a light. To teach Jake to regularly use the new room as a place to calm down, Jake's therapist gave Jim suggestions for words and phrases. To Jim, the therapist's approach seemed counterintuitive, but he tried it anyway. And it worked. During a major tantrum, Jim was able to get his son to go in the quiet room and stay there until he calmed down. Jim would wait outside reading a book. Sometimes it took up to 3 hours, but Jim was persistent. After a couple of months, there were noticeably fewer tantrums, and they became shorter in length. This ultimately led to fewer tantrums at school, allowing Jim to put in full work days most of the time. Plus, Jim began to have hope for his son and their lives together.

A persistent parent, Tracy and her son Trevor

When Tracy's son and daughter were young, there were no problems and life was good. But very gradually, her son Trevor's behavior became more and more disruptive, and as his troubles worsened, Tracy was drawn in to spending all her time and energy on him. By Trevor's 8th birthday, Tracy's formerly strong marriage was on the rocks because of disagreements with her husband about how to handle their son. Further, she was criticized and avoided by her sister, who blamed Tracy for Trevor' behavior. Someone finally told Tracy to get her son psychological help. The child psychologist who evaluated Trevor determined that he probably had both PDD (pervasive development disorder, with multiple learning disabilities) and a low enough IQ to be considered developmentally disabled. The lower-then-average IQ was especially discouraging, because it meant Trevor might never be able to respond to behavior modification therapies. He wouldn't be able to control himself, or understand lessons, or learn proper behavior. Tracy arranged every possible intervention, from medication, to improved diet, to exercise, to special therapies; each helped but only a little. She and her husband faced a lifetime of intensive support for their son.

Tracy got some therapy for herself and occasionally visited a support group. She eventually brought her reluctant husband to the support group, which really helped him overcome negative attitudes towards Trevor and his desire to punish his son. Next, Tracy's support group helped her recognize that her daughter, Tina, had emerging problems: nightmares, panic attacks, crying for no apparent reason, were possibly all signs of PTSD. Then seeking help for Tina, Tracy discovered Tina had endured bullying and attacks from her brother that Tracy hadn't noticed before. She sought and received help for

Tina, who has since lost her fears and nightmares and returned to being herself, happy and with lots of friends.

A parent who balanced her children's needs, Marie and her daughters Megan and Monica

Marie was a single mom with two daughters, both vibrant and talented, and they made her very proud. Her eldest, 14-year-old Megan, earned high test scores on national exams. But one day, Megan came home from school crying, with all D's and F's on her report card. She explained that she couldn't hear the teacher because of voices in her head, and that words moved around on the blackboard. The family doctor immediately referred Megan to a child psychiatrist, who suspected schizophrenia. Over the following year, Marie watched helplessly as Megan's personality turned negative and she began acting bizarrely. Many medications were tried, but each had an uncomfortable side effect so there were constant changes. Megan became impatient with taking medications because they made her feel nauseous and "weird;" and she accused Marie and the psychiatrist of trying to control her.

During this period, Marie started falling apart. She was overwhelmed by fear for Megan's well being, and by grief at the "death" of Megan's personality. Marie fell into a deep depression and had thoughts of suicide. Marie found a therapist who understood her, because the therapist's own daughter was mentally ill. With help from the therapist and an antidepressant medication, Marie began to conquer her inner demons and face life again. She renewed contact with her ex-husband and convinced him to overcome differences so they could work together for the sake of their daughters. (He had originally blamed Marie for Megan's problems.) They started communicating better than when they were married!

Megan was placed in residential care for five months. During that period, Marie and her other daughter, Monica, attended a therapy session without Megan. In this session, Marie heard how angry and stressed the younger sister had become. It was a shock to Marie, because Monica had always been so positive and encouraging. Monica had been the little cheerleader and support person for both her sister, Megan, and her mother—too much responsibility for a young person of 12! While Megan was in care, Marie made a point of spending quality time with Monica. They went on fun mother-daughter adventures, and Monica was allowed to invite friends over for slumber parties. This was not possible when Megan was around. These activities set Monica free to be a young preteen instead of a little adult. The renewed bond between Marie and Monica help them support each other once Megan returned home.

Megan left residential care practically cured! This lasted a few months until she renewed friendships with other troubled teens in the community, began taking meds sporadically, and started blaming her parents for her problems. For a couple of years, she was able to attend college part time and achieve excellent grades, yet each term ended in a breakdown, and each breakdown was worse, resulting in hospitalization. Megan eventually stopped taking all medications and became paranoid and angry; she endured homelessness, assaults, and periods of drug use. She fought every attempt her parents made to help her out.

At 25, and severely psychotic, the local mental health authority held Megan in a psychiatric hospital for 3 weeks before she could leave. While there, for the first time in years, Megan was on medication and capable of looking back on her troubled life. Megan met other patients in the unit who were nice to her, and who told her that she was OK, just that had a problem in her brain that was not her fault. Megan changed her attitude. She welcomed both her mother and father in therapy and told them she was making a commitment to staying on her medications, and that she wanted to restart the life that "ended" years before.

An anxious controlling parent who learned to relax, Mike and his son Matthew

Mike and his wife, Margery, had been married many years and had two sons, Mitch and Matthew, who were 8 years apart in age. Because Margery had a high-paying job and a busy travel schedule, Mike opted to work out of the home and raise their two sons. The eldest, Mitch, grew profoundly negative and cynical about life in his late teens, and committed suicide. Both parents and Matthew were utterly devastated. Margery and Mike felt overwhelming guilt at not recognizing Mitch's depression nor seeking help. The younger son Matthew or "Matt," was 8 at the time, and was consoled by his parents as best as they could. Starting around age 10, Matt became defiant at home, and by 11 he started to cause problems at school. By 12, Matt's grades fell sharply and he was accused of an act of vandalism at a neighbor's.

Matt's parents profoundly feared that history would repeat itself—another troubled son, another suicide. They would not make the same mistake again! Mike went after treatment for Matt with a vengeance, making lots of phone calls and placing incessant demands on therapists, counselors, and teachers. They sympathized, but they dreaded his many daily calls. Mike read everything he could to diagnose Matt himself, and he pressured a doctor into prescribing medications for his son. Mike's intense anxiety and need to "fix" his son fed his tendency to clamp down on Matt at home, which aggravated the situation. By 13, Matt's defiance and behavior worsened. He stole a motorcycle, and crashed it, and ended up in the emergency room.

No one was certain, but Mike assumed this was a suicide attempt and demanded psychiatric treatment and residential care once Matt was out of the hospital. And he got it. At the residential care facility, the staff determined that Matt's defiance issues were treatable with a traditional combination of therapies: talk therapy, exercise, a different school curriculum (Matt had a mild learning disability), and a low dose of an antidepressant. The real problem was that his father Mike, though well-intentioned, was creating an atmosphere that overtaxed his son's compromised ability to cope, and Matt would probably go downhill again once back at home.

Mike's anxiety required a lot of patience from the many staff working with Matt, but the son's therapist finally convinced Mike to get his own therapy to address his anxiety and remaining grief and guilt over Mitch. Mike eventually calmed down enough to understand that Matt's situation was not as serious as Mitch's and that it was treatable, but that he had to learn new ways to interact with his son. After Matt's discharge, it took two years of outpatient therapy with father and son together to rebuild the relationship, gain trust, and learn new ways of communicating, but it worked. Matt is nearing his senior year in high school and doing well, and the family is at peace at home.

A bullied parent who took back control, Hannah and her daughter Heather

Hannah had a strong, stable, financially comfortable marriage with four children, three boys and a deeply troubled oldest daughter, Heather. At 16, Heather had been diagnosed with borderline personality disorder and possibly bipolar disorder. Heather was relentlessly verbally abusive and manipulative, and Hannah became worn down from trying to control her own anger at her daughter, and depressed over her inability to protect her three sons from their sister's vicious anger. Hannah's husband was supportive, but he was also away for long periods on business. The extended family and friends were also sympathetic and supportive, but this still could not protect everyone from

Heather's unremitting abuse. She had bullied everyone into submission and was in complete control of the household.

An unexpected suicide attempt got Heather to an emergency room, then brief hospitalization in a psychiatric ward, and a referral to a few weeks in psychiatric residential care. Ironically, Hannah was relieved instead of upset. She and her family got some needed respite, and the emotional space to cope with pent up anxiety in family therapy (without Heather). The therapist in the residential program saw through an attempt by Heather to paint herself as a victim of her family's abuse, and the therapist confronted Heather in front of her mother. Hannah was never able to do this, but she observed her daughter comply instead of threaten, and she realized she probably had more authority to set rules than she thought.

She found a family support group that included other parents with hyper-emotional teen girls with similar challenges. Meeting the other parents helped Hannah overcome self-doubt about her abilities as a parent, and guilt from the many instances she lost her temper and yelled at Heather. One mother pointed out that it was essential to take back control and stand up to one's child without giving in. Another empathized with the painful side of raising a daughter like Heather. This parent philosophized that it was important to accept that Heather may never improve or recover, and that she might head for disaster despite Hannah making every effort to prevent this.

Within a short time, the affirmations from other parents helped Hannah feel the return of her former spunk and energy. Emotionally, she let go of her daughter, and forgave herself, and put her energy into her sons. Heather's transition to adulthood was a series of crises (periods of drug use, promiscuity, and STD's), but Hannah was able to face each crisis without the intense pain as before. She eventually found humor in situations, and joy in those rare sparkling moments when Heather was happy and affectionate. She said she would be more at peace should anything tragic happen to Heather—as there was always the possibility of suicide. Hannah eventually offered to mentor other parents with similar difficult teen daughters, and she experienced the deep gratification that comes from helping others.

A parent who successfully used structure, Deanne and her son Danny

Deanne was a survivor of domestic abuse from her ex-husband. She left their home to escape him, and took their two children out of state with her, a boy of 13 and a girl of 7. Like many who escape violence at home and flee quickly, she left everything behind: job, belongings, friends, and moved in with her mother to start life anew. Deanne was excited to start over and reinvent herself, and she was determined enough to pull it off, but her son Danny did everything he could to thwart her. He refused to go to school; he played destructive pranks on neighbors so that Deanne and her children were evicted from her mother's apartment. Danny would relentlessly tease his sister, Debra, so Deanne had to watch constantly or arrange costly day care for Debra to protect her. Danny stole his mother's purse and destroyed her ID. To harass her, he screamed whenever Deanne was on the phone, or he'd pull the cord from the wall. Deanne struggled to attend vocational classes to get a new career, but after a year and a half her grades went from A's to D's because of the many times she had to skip class to deal with Danny problems, and then blow her assignments. Danny pulled a new prank one day to upset his mother; he set a fire in their apartment. No one was hurt, but Danny immediately entered the juvenile justice and mental health system. Deanne was again evicted, but the fire incident was a blessing in disguise.

Danny was required to attend special "firesetter" classes and get individual and family therapy, and he was admitted to a day school program where he was continuously monitored and limited to strict boundaries. (This day school offered special secure transport so Danny couldn't escape or refuse to go.) Deanne learned through the family therapist and a support group how to change her whole approach to parenting Danny, and she made a complete turnaround—she began to work on improving home life rather than improving Danny. First, Deanne had to accept the inconveniences. She put a lock on her bedroom and stored all important belongings there; she removed the lock on the bathroom door so Danny couldn't lock himself in and spread shampoo all over the mirror. She had Debra sleep on a cot in her bedroom to be safe from Danny, and got expensive cell phone service so she could make calls without interruption. She made many physical changes to prevent Danny from seriously disrupting the household.

At home and at school, changing Danny's environment, 24 and 7, started to change Danny. He remained immature, behaving more like a 9-year-old by his 14th birthday, but his behavior vastly improved and, after two years, Danny started to attend public school again, where his behavior was only occasionally a problem. At home, Deanne was able to control him better, too, and saw fewer and fewer disruptions. Her work with Danny and her experiences with his treatment inspired her to begin a new career, and she entered the mental health services program at her school. After Deanne's graduation, she moved into a career with a county mental health agency.

∾

We live in hopeful times for those with mental disorders. The 1990's were the Decade of the Brain. For the first time in history, we finally had the technology to measure and understand the fleeting interactions between chemicals and neurons in the brain. We could look inside a living brain and see where the active regions were when a person was doing a given task. We could look at electrical activity, blood flow, and trace the intricate chemical pathway from when a person sees something, and where the visual message goes to cause their reaction. With this information, researchers have since found ways to improve brain function by designing complex molecules for medicines. Others have used these technological tools to rapidly diagnose a disorder and devise therapies to help the person.

To me, the greatest discoveries came from studies that looked at adults who successfully recovered from their symptoms; studies that asked what was going on in their lives to support them. Again and again, the answers rested on the people in their lives—the people that showed them how to manage their unusual perceptions; the ones that added or eliminated foods or medications in their diet; the ones that showed love and acceptance and belief in them. This is where you come in.

Anticipate natural changes in your child's life. Your troubled son or daughter will go through stages of awareness and development as do other children their age, and each stage brings a new, difficult behavior. At each stage, you must make adjustments to managing your child, and this could mean lots of new changes in your household. **All you need is to stay one step ahead** of your child's next stage, to keep your sanity and ensure that your family thrives as best they can.

These are *generalizations* of stages in the development of a troubled child, and the issues you face as a parent:

Age 3- 5+, entering school:

If your child is diagnosed at this stage or clearly troubled, get as much help as possible *now*. Your child's brain is not yet mature, and early treatment can and does improve them. With luck and hard work, they will be ready for adulthood by the time they are 18. Since your child is young, there are usually lots of services for them in schools or "special needs" programs. (If you are reluctant to have your child labeled "special needs" at this young age, and are put off by this term, I encourage you to set this aside and seek whatever services are available. "Special needs" was formerly used for children who were retarded or developmentally disabled, but the meaning now includes any child with a disability. It does not imply your child is of low intelligence.)

Roughly age 8 to 11:

Your child is bigger and more capable of disruption, which is a problem if they are aggressive or destructive to themselves or others. They are starting to pick up new ideas and behaviors that aren't as easy to cope with as before. Fewer services are available, and you might need to make extra efforts to obtain them, such as an Individual Education Plan (IEP), and you may need help from a mental health specialist rather than a pediatrician.

Age 11-13, entering adolescence and puberty:

In general, the more serious mental disorders start to manifest in early adolescence. The sudden changes in your child's behavior can be unbelievably upsetting. Pay attention to feelings of grief caused by sensing the loss of your child's previous self. Their true self is not lost, just hidden.

At this stage, there are fewer supportive programs available in schools and in the community, and more emphasis on punishment. Your child/teen might be impossible to protect or manage physically, they start showing ingrained patterns of behaviors, and they are more open to negative influences from friends and other adults. You are entering a difficult period. From now until young adulthood, your main goal will be to keep them in school and out of trouble, and consistently receiving mental health treatment.

Age 13 to 17 (and into the 20's) are the most dangerous and risky years:

Pace yourself for a marathon. You have many important tasks: consistent treatment, maintaining trust and communication, taking care of yourself and family, creating a therapeutic home, and keeping your expectations realistic. First and foremost, reduce stressors. Consider all options for stress reduction, such as delaying school completion. Put lots of energy in intensive structure and boundary setting. Get all medical records before age 18 when you'll no longer have access without their permission.

Age 18, "partial" adulthood:

Your teen is still not an adult per se, and probably still dependent on your family. They can refuse medication and treatment, but they can't demand to be in your home anymore, as you are not legally bound to provide care. Ironically, some families find it easier to set boundaries at this stage, and get more cooperation and respect from their child. In my opinion, this may be because the parent feels more comfortable being assertive, or perhaps the child is more aware of how dependent they still are on the parent, and is more willing to cooperate.

Age 21

It's time for you to transition from parenting to supporting. They will have begun to settle into set patterns of behavior that are typical of their diagnosis, and they will face a series of life challenges created by those patterns. This time is when they start on their own path, and become who they are to become. Be a constant for them, a positive supporter, a guide, a mentor, and most of all, a sympathetic listener.

Plan for a long bumpy ride. Your child will concern you well into their adulthood, but this needn't drain you or your resources if you have a long-term view and maintain your support network. Look for gradual improvement in stability over the years, but expect scary events that will test your faith. There will be periods when your child seems recovered, but you must still stay alert. Anything can happen: a stressful event, a series of nights without sleep, skipped doses of medications, relationship stress... and your child can head downhill. Stay watchful and communicate with them often. Keep a bridge open. Don't give up on them! **Research shows that a support net truly makes a difference in a person's long term prognosis and recovery—be part of that support net!**

<u>The Ten Principles of Support *</u>

1. We acknowledge the fact that someone we love has a mental illness.

2. We accept that we have no control over this disorder or the child/adolescent with the disorder. We only have control over our own actions and thoughts.

3. We release all feelings of guilt concerning this mental illness for we are not to blame for the disorder or its effects.

4. We understand and acknowledge that the mental illness has had an impact on all of our relationships.

5. We forgive ourselves for mistakes we have made and we forgive others for wrongs we feel have been committed against us.

6. We choose to be happy and healthy. We choose to return to a healthy focus on ourselves.

7. We keep our expectations for ourselves and for our child/adolescent with a mental illness at realistic levels.

8. We believe that we have inner resources, which will help us with our own growth and will sustain us through crisis.

9. We acknowledge the strength and value of this support system and we commit ourselves to sustaining it for our benefit and the benefit of other families.

10. We acknowledge that there is a higher power to whom we will turn to nurture and strengthen our ability to release control over the things we cannot control.

* National Alliance on Mental Illness (NAMI)

Appendix – Sources of information

Family Medical Leave Act - FMLA
By federal law, employers are required to offer up to 12 weeks leave per year to an employee with a child or dependent with a chronic disability.

- The **leave can be taken weekly, daily, or hourly** as needed, up to 480 hours per year. It can include doctor's appointments or other transport to care.
- **Employees are entitled to leave to care for a medically needy or disabled child**, which may include direct supervision of the child in a situation where they cannot be left alone, but not for daycare or babysitting. *Children with mental and emotional disorders satisfy the criteria for a medical disability.*

Under FMLA, employees must work for a firm with 50 or more employees and have worked there at least 1 year. Individual states often have their own family leave laws, which can be more generous. My own state of Oregon has a family leave act that covers parents in a firm with only 25 or more employees and only 6 months employment.

Two reasons to consider getting an attorney

Plan to make a will to preserve funds for your child's benefit, and to limit their access to money that they cannot use rationally. In the will, create a section for an **Irrevocable Trust** that names your child as the beneficiary. The money is theirs, but *only* a trustee whom you designate is allowed to provide it to them, and the trustee must follow certain rules:

What the funds can be used for: Real property such as a home or condo (including maintenance and repairs), education, household goods, travel, professional services (such as medical or dental care, hair cuts, and tax preparation), phone and Internet charges, and a car or bicycle.

What funds cannot be used for: food, rent, clothing, and basic utilities.

The Irrevocable Trust was specifically created for people with mental challenges such as the developmentally disabled and sufferers of Alzheimer's, to prevent the person from misusing the money or being taken advantage of. This is not only for wealthy people; even a few thousand dollars can help your child with beneficial things like classes or transportation for a long time.

Next, you will need an attorney specialized in disabilities law to designate someone to make legal decisions on behalf of your child. This designee needs to be given **Power of Attorney** and **Guardianship** to make financial and medical decisions if your child is not competent to make reasoned decisions for themselves.

Psychiatric Advanced Directive

A psychiatric advanced directive is a document your child can sign that gives someone else the right to hospitalize them if your child becomes psychotic and might otherwise refuse to go. If your child is approaching age 18, and you have their understanding and trust, they can sign this and appoint you as the decision maker, which is called giving you "power of attorney." More about these directives can found online from the Bazelon Center for Mental Health Law, www.bazelon.org.

What is "commitment"?

If your child becoming psychotic and/or dangerous and refuses both medication and psychiatric hospitalization, you may want to get them committed against their will. Only a judge or local mental health authority can decide to force hospitalization. Thirty-seven states in the United States have involuntary commitment laws for people with mental illness. But this is a tricky action. Commitment takes away your child's legal rights to freedom, as if they are being arrested or jailed without cause. Even if your child is under 18, he or she has the right to an attorney to defend themselves against forced hospitalization! Why would they do this? It's common for a psychotic person not to recognize they are sick, and to believe others are trying to control them or hurt them. Be prepared with options if the government mental health authority refuses to commit your child even though you *know* they are not OK.

At the time of this writing, commitment is difficult to obtain because it is so controversial. But if your child is indeed hospitalized against their will, then once they improve enough to be discharged, they must sign a contract or "commitment." This contract states they will stay on medication and see a doctor or therapist regularly for a period of months (90 days to 180 days), or they will be forced back into the hospital again. It's like parole, where the criminal must check-in with a parole officer or go back to prison.

Children under 18 can refuse medication. Many mental health providers respect their young patient's wishes if there is no evidence of impending harm. This might seem very wrong to you! You should request advice from providers for what to do if you think your child is in danger of self-harm or harm to others, because they aren't on medications. And get a second opinion. Be aware that under our laws, they have the right to refuse, and you might need a very different approach to caring for them!

How might you avoid this in the first place? Start now to build trust and cooperation with your child. A truly excellent book for helping you to help your child to accept treatment is: "I'm Not Sick, I Don't Need Help – How to Help Someone with Mental Illness Accept Treatment" by Dr. Xavier Amador, Vida Press, 2007.

Medical IRA

Like the retirement IRA, a Medical IRA allows you to put savings in an account for medical expenses, and get a tax credit for the full amount (your income is reduced by the amount you put in for that year). It is an attractive way to save because you reduce your taxes at the same time.

Websites:

I've reviewed these websites and online support groups, and believe they offer sound guidance for families with a child or adolescent with a mental or emotional disorder. All feature:
- Treatment practices for children and teens that are based on research;
- Email newsletters and research articles with current information and events;
- Directories for support groups and care providers;
- Online forums for parents/family members to ask questions and share stories.

BIPOLAR DISORDER

http://www.bpkids.org/
> An excellent site for bipolar children but access is not free. Users must donate $40 to the Child & Adolescent Bipolar Foundation. It has answers to questions about medical and psychiatric treatments and medications, an online support group, a nationwide directory of support groups and treatment providers, stories about famous people with bipolar disorder, and children's art gallery.

http://health.groups.yahoo.com/group/ParentsofBi-Polars/ - Online support group
> This is a free online discussion list for parents of children and adolescents with Bipolar Disorder. Contributors share information about things they've learned, or simply their trials and joys. One must sign up with Yahoo to join but it is secure and you won't get ads or spam.

ANXIETY DISORDERS

http://www.childanxiety.net/
> The Child Anxiety Network site provides thorough, user-friendly information about child anxiety and a free email newsletter. There are listings for providers, recommended books, "coping cards", and articles with practical parenting tips. This is a good place to start for those who are not sure where to turn when they think their child may need professional help to cope with anxiety

GENERAL CHILDREN'S MENTAL HEALTH

http://www.aboutourkids.org/ (also in Spanish)
> Aboutourkids.org is easy to search for research on multiple childhood psychiatric disorders and has a free email newsletter for parents. It is operated by a children's psychiatric research clinic and there's information on treatment methods, medications, and brain function. It will be especially helpful for those interested in the science behind their child's condition.

http://childparenting.about.com/od/psychologicaldisorders/

The childparenting.com website has dozens of links to information about children's health, ages Kindergarten through 6th grade. At the children's mental health link, the disorders listed below are covered. One could spend a lot of time here and learn much about behavior, discipline, games, and activities. There are links to online parent support groups.

http://www.remedyfind.com/

Highly recommended: RemedyFind is an independent, unbiased site where you can rate the effectiveness of treatments for specific health problems, and the mental health section is very informative regarding medications. It offers informative free email newsletters for different disorders that include information for both children and adults. 1) Find the treatments which have been rated as the most effective for specific health conditions / concerns. 2) Find which treatments are the most effective ones of their type; find the most highly rated treatments by type.

ADD/ADHD

http://www.additudemag.com/additude.asp

AdditudeMag.com is a fun site with lots of practical information and inspiration for parents with children with attention deficit disorders, from how to work with teachers; effective therapies, and play ideas.

www.chadd.org (also in Spanish) - Children & Adults with Attention Deficit/ Hyperactivity Disorder

Chadd.org is an excellent site for exploring a wealth of AD/HD knowledge. Family membership is $45 which includes Attention Magazine, news, advocacy information, stories about celebrities with AD/HD and much more.

ASPERGER's, Autism Spectrum Disorders (ASD)

http://www.asperger.org/

This website is dedicated to providing information and advice to families of children with more advanced autism, high functioning autism, Asperger's Syndrome and pervasive developmental disorder (PDD), which describes children and adolescents within the autism spectrum who do not experience severe intellectual impairments. It offers links to an email newsletter, books, support groups, conferences, and direct links to psychiatric research programs in Autism and Asperger's at Cambridge University, England, and Stanford University, California.

OBSESSIVE COMPULSIVE DISORDER

http://understanding_ocd.tripod.com/ocd_parents.html
This webpage is for parents with a child with OCD symptoms and covers a broad range of topics: FAQs, treatment, medications, therapists, books, etc with links for more information.

BORDERLINE PERSONALITY DISORDER (BPD)

These free discussion groups for parents and siblings were created by the authors of "Stop Walking on Eggshells," Paul Mason and Randi Kreiger, and are especially appropriate for those just beginning to learn about BPD.

ParentsOfBPs
For parents of children (of any age) who may have BPD
Subscribe: WTOParentsofBPs-subscribe@yahoogroups.com
or visit the homepage at: http://groups.yahoo.com/group/WTOParentsOfBPs

Siblings
For siblings of a person with BP
Subscribe: WTOSibling-subscribe@yahoogroups.com
or visit the homepage at: http://groups.yahoo.com/group/WTOSibling

(For privacy, the site recommends creating a confidential e-mail address at www.yahoo.com before subscribing, and to consider subscribing to the digest to avoid 25-100 emails a day.)

DEPRESSION

http://www.dbsalliance.org/ (also in Spanish)
The Depression and Bipolar Support Alliance (DBSA) has an excellent site for both children and adults and it is easy-to-use. It offers information

on symptoms and medications, directories to providers, clinical trials and research, as well as chat groups, and e-newsletter, and online forums.

http://www.familyaware.org/teenguides.php

This is a page on the Families for Depression Awareness website (www.familyaware.org) that offers free downloads of two excellent guides: one for teens with depression and one for parents of teens and children with depression. These guides are for families with children who are already diagnosed with depression (not bipolar disorder) and are in treatment (in talk therapy and/or taking antidepressants). There is help here for any member of a family affected by depression.

CONDUCT DISORDERS

http://www.conductdisorders.com/ (translation available in Spanish)

This is a family-friendly and supportive site with a lot of information that is easy to find: articles, books, forums, links, plus information on most other childhood psychiatric disorders, not just conduct disorders. A parent newsletter is not available, but it is still a great site overall.

POST TRAUMATIC STRESS DISORDER

http://www.ptsdalliance.org

The PTSD Alliance website is easy to navigate and provides clear concise information about PTSD in adults and children for the purpose of education, and it is helpful for parents or guardians of children with PTSD. They offer two free downloadable booklets on PTSD, answers to FAQs, provider listings, and information about how to work with providers

෴

www.raisingtroubledkids.com

My own website features lots of information and links, and is not specialized for any given disorder. It includes a blog, and I strongly encourage contributions. Your stories can provide a constant source of new and practical ideas for how to raise a troubled child.

Hang in there.

Made in the USA
Las Vegas, NV
14 November 2022